Men of Schiff
A History of the Professional Scouters Who Built the Boy Scouts of America

Men of Schiff
A History of the Professional Scouters Who Built the Boy Scouts of America

By Winston R. Davis

ISBN 978-0-578-11283-1

In Memory of Don Owens, Ike Sutton and especially, Bill Hillcourt.

Men of Schiff Together

Men of Schiff together
Taking to the world
Scouting ways forever
Flags and banners mightily unfurled

To our Oath and Scout Law
True we'll always be
With every Council
Every Region
Bound together in our legion
Men of Schiff are we.

Acknowledgements

While there have been many people who have encouraged me, helped me and, from time to time, nagged me, about getting this book written, special thanks is due to some.

Thanks to the archivists and curators of the Seton Library and Philmont Museum at Philmont Scout Ranch, Cimmaron, New Mexico. In 2007, I made a stop at Philmont for old time's sake. I hadn't been there in many years and just wanted to see how the place had changed. I visited the library and museum and found a goldmine of books and literature about historical Scouting. So I stayed over a couple of days just to work in the library and got enough information to make a list of books and authors. I started acquiring books, mainly council histories, from which I could begin to put together information. I do not, unfortunately, have the names of those who helped me during those days.

My next stop was Irving, Texas, where I met Steven Price, the diligent archivist of the National Scouting Museum, who has provided me with some invaluable assistance over the years since. This past year, I encountered Corry Kanzenberg, Curator of Collections and Exhibits at the museum, who offered further assistance, at the National Meeting in Orlando.

I must thank the late Wayne Kempton and his wife Caroline, long-time Scouting friends, who brought back my first council history from Nashville many years ago. I also owe a debt of gratitude to Jim Foster, a really long-time Scouting friend, for giving me a major part of his collection of memorabilia from Schiff Scout Reservation. And, thanks to Jim Colvert, who gave me a copy of William D. Murray's *The History of the Boy Scouts of America*, a reliable volume of the early history of Scouting. Thanks to my old Scouting friend John Cox, who read my manuscript and made suggestions for improvement.

Thanks to Ray Matoy, who sent me encouragement and a story, and to the late Dick Newcomb, who spent over an hour on the phone with me from his home in Roswell, talking about his experiences. Thanks to Kenn Drupiewski, my old boss, who shared some of his perspectives on a life in professional Scouting and his thoughts about a book on professional Scouting.

Special thanks to Marylou Gantner, who has been my inspiration since I started toying with the idea of writing. She has always told me I was supposed to write this little history.

And, of course, thanks to all the men, named and nameless, who wrote the histories of their councils for posterity and thus made this information available.

Table of Contents

Preface

This book is written as a memorial. It is dedicated to the long line of men and women who, between 1910 and the present, have served as members of the legion of professional Scouters.

The song, *Men of Schiff,* was written by a now forgotten man who was attending the National Training School at Mortimer L. Schiff Scout Reservation in New Jersey.[1] Schiff was the 400 acre park-like setting in which thousands of men, and a small number of women were trained in how to become professional employees of the Boy Scouts of America. They came from all over the United States to spend a few weeks learning the history and methods of professional Boy Scouting. Many, if not most, had been Scouts and adult leaders of Scouts. Between 1932 and 1979, Schiff was the main training ground for them. Only in the middle 1970s were women were admitted to their ranks.

The National Training School, later called the National Executive Institute, for professionals, was not the only training that took place at Schiff. The highest level of training for volunteer and professional Scout leaders, called Wood Badge, was created at Gilwell Park, outside London, by an experienced group of British Scouters, including the Founder of Boy Scouting, Robert Baden-Powell, in 1919. It was tried at Schiff in 1936, but the top leadership thought it "too British" and it was not until 1948 that the first American Wood Badge course was held at Schiff Scout Reservation with William Hillcourt as Scoutmaster.

Much more is to be said about Hillcourt, but he was an important figure in the growth of Boy Scouting in the United States. National Wood Badge courses were held at Schiff until it was closed in 1979.

In the 1960s, a national training course for boy leaders was begun at Schiff. For two weeks, boys from all around the country spent two weeks living in camp and learning skills to help them be better leaders and trainers of other boys. The course, called National Junior Leader Instructor Training Camp, was held throughout the summers and hundreds, if not thousands, of boys attended.

William Hillcourt lived at Schiff Scout Reservation in its early years and ran a Boy Scout troop there, with boys from the local area as members. Hillcourt learned how American Scouting really worked at a practical level and used his experience to write essential guides for boy and adult leaders in Scouting.

Many other special events took place on those beautiful grounds. Lord Baden-Powell, Founder of Scouting, visited and his wife Olave, Lady Baden-Powell, continued to visit long after his death. Many Scouting notables from around the world came there to share their knowledge with trainees in the various schools over the years.

Schiff was an old country estate with a manor house that had been donated to the Boy Scouts of America in the 1920s as a training place. It was a big tract of land with pleasant cottages and classroom buildings gathered around a lake with docks for swimming and boating.

Schiff was a beautiful place, filled with legend and lore of the Boy Scouts of America. It seemed to stand for Boy Scouting itself. Its history and importance to the development of Boy Scouting seemed to make it obvious that "Men of Schiff" was an appropriate way to describe the legions of professional Scouters who went there for nearly fifty years. Thus, it became the title of this book.

Since the foundation of the Boy Scouts of America, there have been thousands of professional Scouters who have worked long hours, including many weekends, assisting, guiding and directing the millions of men and women volunteers who make Scouting possible.

This book is intended to set down a few of the stories of these people, not only for them, but for their families and for future generations to understand what motivated us. Although I left professional Scouting many years ago to pursue a different career, I still consider many of these professionals and former professionals to have been among my closest friends. I hope to be able to portray the quality of some of these men in these pages.

The author has been a registered member of the Boy Scouts of America for more than sixty years, first as Cub Scout, then as a Boy Scout. As an adult, I have served as a Scoutmaster, Sea Scout Skipper, Commissioner, Commodore and a few other positions. I was fortunate enough to meet and talk with many Scouting notables and non notables. I had the privilege of being a personal friend of William L. "Green Bar Bill" Hillcourt, a professional who had great impact on the development of the Boy Scout program, during the last years of his long life. I have traveled much and met Scouters from all around the world along the way, both professional and non professional.

As a longtime, dedicated Scouter, I've felt for some years that this is a book that needs to be written. My hope is that it will appeal to many readers who were never a part of Scouting, never knew any professional Scouters and possibly never guessed there was such a career. I feel that they, along with those who have known and worked with these dedicated men and women, will recognize their dedication and love of

Scouting. Hopefully, most will share interest in the historical aspects of the early years when these "Men of Schiff" built a movement out of nothing but a book written by an English general, the interest of boys and the willingness of men like fictional Lem Siddons of MacKinlay Kantor's great book *For God and My Country*, later a movie called *Follow Me Boys*, to take on the job of teaching boys to love the outdoors and live comfortably there.[2]

Although the book is primarily about the *men* of Schiff, we will not overlook the role of the ladies in Scouting. There have been women in the employ of the BSA from almost the beginning and women have been members of the ranks of professional Scouters since the early 1970s. Today, women play a great role in volunteer leadership of Scouting, but some of the real heroines in the history of Scouting have been the wives of professional Scouters. They have been willing to let their husbands go off to camps for weeks, meetings and training courses for days. They have put up with their absences evenings and weekends as they do their normal jobs and supported them because they believed in the work their spouses were doing. Often, a professional's wife could be found working at an event he was running. There have been many ladies who, as members of an office staff, have in fact run their employers' councils while the men were running summer camps or traveling long distances away from home to recruit and train more volunteers for Scouting.

It has been my intention to write this book for a long time. Now, I hope to share this little slice of history with others. I apologize to my readers in advance for the fact that the book is semi-autobiographical and, written from the author's point of view. I could not come up with a better way to do it and have done my best to keep my ego under control.

Chapter One

Becoming a Professional Scouter

In August 1970, freshly released from active duty in the United States Air Force (although I remained in the Active Reserve until 1995) and hired by the South Florida Council, Boy Scouts of America (BSA) to be the Assistant District Executive of the New River District in Fort Lauderdale, I was duly dispatched to Schiff Scout Reservation in New Jersey for training.

Not long before I joined the ranks of professional Scouters, the Boy Scouts of America had gotten new leadership and was undergoing changes to meet modern times. Along with these changes, the professional training at Schiff, formerly called the National Training School was now designated the National Executive Institute. It was a different curriculum and a different routine for daily life at Schiff.

My class benefited from this by a relaxed regimen at the training school. A couple of years earlier, classes were conducted for men in full Boy Scout uniform who moved from place to place in patrol formation, carrying their flags. They were confined to the reservation for six weeks and attended classes night and day.

In our time, we often wore civilian clothes and could leave the reservation at any time we were not otherwise engaged. They did, however, lock the main gate around midnight, so if you tarried too long at the Three Lights Tavern in nearby Bernardsville, you had to walk in from the gate. Some did tend to spend time at the Three Lights nightly and livelier places on weekends down at Atlantic City.

To me, Schiff was a Scouting Mecca. On the first morning there, we were treated to a group of young Boy Scouts in full uniform from the National Junior Leader Instructor Training Camp, singing the song, *Men of Schiff*, for us in the dining hall. The dark wood-paneled walls were covered with original Norman Rockwell artwork, mostly ones he drew for *Boys Life Magazine* covers. There was a plaque on the grounds to commemorate the 1935 visit of Lord Baden-Powell, Founder of Scouting and another to mark the spot where "Uncle Dan" Beard, a national figure and a founder of Scouting in the U.S., opened the first campfire. While I was there, Olave (pronounced olive), Lady Baden-Powell, widow of the Founder, visited Schiff and spoke with us. Another visitor was William "Green Bar Bill" Hillcourt. I knew him from his monthly columns in *Boys Life Magazine* and later his book, *Baden-Powell, The Two Lives of a Hero*.[3]

He spoke to us in the Memorial Room, its fireplace decorated with ancient Roman marble sculpture, where he recalled Baden-Powell's visit to Schiff and mentioned a reception held in that very room thirty-five years earlier. I was enthralled.

Some of my classmates were less enthralled about the history of Scouting and the place. I was amazed to discover that quite a few members of the class had joined the profession as a job. Some had no idea who Bill Hillcourt was. One of the guys couldn't get his name right and humorously referred to him as "Green Briar Bob." To them, it was a process to go through en route to getting on with business.

Professional Scouting in 1970 was an unusual choice of livelihoods and always was.

We were expected to work a lot of nights and weekends. After all, that's when the boys and the volunteer Scouters are available. For the most part, we didn't keep office hours. I lived in my service area, called a district, which was over an hour's drive from the Scout office in Miami. In one day, you might have breakfast or lunch in a diner with a blue collar volunteer and dine on steak and lobster that night with bank presidents and wealthy lawyers. Our job then was the same as it is now, and as it was in 1910: to raise money to keep the thing going (and pay our salaries), organize Boy Scout troops and Cub Scout packs and recruit and train leaders to run them. The Scout office building in Miami was a modern, up-to-date facility on Coral Way. The one I worked out of in Orlando was a former plant nursery, housed in a metal building, with tiny cubbyholes in which the district men worked.

One of the fun things we did was called "School Night for Scouting." We would go to all the elementary schools in our area, pass out flyers and go from classroom to classroom telling kids to get their parents out that night so they could join Scouting. In the evening, we would hold a meeting in the cafeteria. If a Cub Pack existed at that school, their leaders would be there, we would sign up the kids and that was that. On the other hand, if there was no pack, we would divide everybody up by neighborhood and tell them they had to get together and select one of the parents to be a Den Mother (today, Den Leader, since men can also lead Cub Dens). Pressure was on. One of the men had to stand up and agree to be Cubmaster. The crazy thing was, it usually worked. You had to have the fervor of an evangelist preacher to rouse enough enthusiasm. If you couldn't do that, you wouldn't last long in the business.

One of the not- fun things about Scouting in those days was that we had number goals assigned every year, for boy members in each program and for numbers of units (troops and packs) in each. If you made your goals, you got ahead. If you didn't you got a lot of pressure and eventually you got fired.

This was the result of the program called "Boypower '76," the objective of which was to have one boy out of every three in the United States in Scouting. The goals were assigned from the top down and were often impossible to meet. Sadly, it forced everybody to cheat. There were lots of scandals where people would just create units and register names out of the phone book. Many of these "units" were in minority areas, so the councils could claim also to be serving more minority youth. Over a dozen councils across the country eventually admitted to lying about their figures and using phony units.[4]

Less scandalous, but quite universal, was the practice of taking names of kids from elementary school surveys and signing them up for Cub Scouts. You paid the registration fees out of your own pocket. If you were strictly honest, you sent each kid a postcard saying he had been given a free membership in the Cub Scouts and the phone number of the Cubmaster. Fortunately, those days have passed, but there is still a lot of pressure to grow and of course money has to be raised. An organization that doesn't grow and plan for the future is a dying organization. From the earliest days of Scouting, it was recognized that Scout Executives would always need to plan for the future, but always in an understanding of current conditions.

At the Second Biennial Conference of Boy Scout Executives in 1922, a sales, advertising and merchandising consultant to many big corporations, told the assembled executives, "It is the greatest mistake to think you can get along without (a) proper system, adequate records, budgeting, without some scientific forecasting as to what you are going to do, and how and when and where it can be done."[5]

In the late Sixties and early Seventies, the leadership of the BSA just overlooked or overestimated the "how and when and where *it can be done*" part of that.

Out of a given group of boys, a certain number will become Cubs, Scouts or join programs for older youth. A certain number will not or will be unable to. You can increase numbers through sales, like any business, but there is a point at which boys just aren't interested or can't find a Scout unit they like.

Another fun thing was summer camp. In my first council, we junior people took turns helping out at camp for a week of summer camp.

My first summer at Camp Sebring, near the town of racing fame, we had forest fires every day. In Florida, during a drought, fires crop up from lightening, or from kids with matches, all the time. You can put them out, but the roots smolder underground and then break out again.

We had a sort of fire truck with a pump and water reservoir. When the fire gong rang, the whole staff would drop whatever they were doing and race out to the fire, pulling this wheeled contraption by hand. We had rakes, shovels and a tool like a rake handle with a big flap of rubber on the end to beat out the flames.

Of course, the temperatures were in the high nineties and the humidity was 98 percent. You would get filthy and sweat-soaked, so you went back to your cabin, took a shower and put on clean clothes. An hour later the gong would ring again. Fortunately, we were all very young and had a sense of humor.

Camp staffs in Boy Scout camps are mostly teenagers. A lot are high school students and some are college age. They were a lot of fun to work with, but they could be very irresponsible. There was a girls' camp not far away and mutual, unsupervised, visits were not uncommon. They also had a tendency to throw their camp leaders into the lake occasionally. If they liked you, they would hold your wallet for you. If they didn't, everything went. I got to be director of an aquatic camp that summer before I went off to New Jersey. I really enjoyed that part of Scouting. I had been a camp staffer while in college, so I knew a little about what went on among the young staff. My research for this book has shown me that things were not very different in the first half of the Twentieth Century. A few camp episodes from the distant past will be related as we go through history.

One of my summer camp experiences was seminal. In 1972, the South Florida Council was scheduled to open the McGregor Smith Scout Reservation near Wildwood, Florida.[6] It's a long way from Miami, but land was cheaper and they had bought enough of it to expand for many years. The senior leadership of the council hired a close friend of mine who was a key volunteer in my district to be the initial camp director. He made it a condition of his employment that I be his assistant. I had a lot of summer camp experience, but this one was entirely different.

The land the camp was on had been cattle ranches for more than a hundred years. Behind what became one of the campsites, we found the decayed remains of a cattle-dipping station from the late 19th Century. There had been a widespread disease in those years and cattle were rounded up and eventually run through a concrete trench filled with some kind of liquid to stop the disease. To build the camp, they had to construct roads, clear areas for camp sites and construct buildings and latrines. Thanks to an early hurricane and the usual construction delays, the camp was not finished on time. The staff went up there only about a week ahead of time and we were amazed to find how much remained to be done. We worked our behinds off and still, when the troops started arriving on Sunday, everything was just not ready.

Oh, and did I mention that a major thunderstorm struck almost every afternoon?

On the first Sunday check-in day of the season, many troops were shown to their campsites, which contained boxes of tents and stacks of platforms. Normally, these are all set up with bunks inside and the leaders and boys just move in. At McGregor Smith that year, you got to build your own campsite! Some of the sites didn't have running water yet. Except what was coming down from above, of course.

To my surprise, most of the leaders accepted all this with no fuss and made the best of a bad situation. Of course, the heavy rain made it all a nightmare. At least we staff members had dry places to sleep with bathrooms and running water, but we were exhausted. By Monday (or maybe Tuesday), things were almost working everywhere and most of the troops had a pleasant week at camp. There is an axiom among long-time Scout leaders: Never go to camp the first week or the last week of the season.

During the week before the kids arrived and off and on thru the summer, we found poisonous snakes everywhere. Most were rattlers, but there were also moccasins and coral snakes.

The snakes lived among the palmetto roots which had grown to an amazing size in a hundred years and when the bush hogs came and dug it all up, the snakes had to find new living quarters. A lot of these snakes were six feet long and more. As humorist Dave Barry would say, I am not making this up.[7] We senior adults carried pistols around in our vehicles to dispatch the reptiles if necessary. Nobody got bitten by snakes. Everybody got bitten by the soccer ball sized mosquitoes. Mosquito nets were mandatory in the tents. There were also wild pigs all over the place. They retreated pretty quickly after the campers moved in, but you would see them crossing the roads and dashing into the brush.

Did I mention it was hot? South Florida is quite pleasant in the summer because there are sea breezes down there to moderate the temperature, like an island.

Central Florida is different. The ocean breezes don't get too far inland, so the high temperatures and humidity really wear you down. Since it was a modern camp, we had air-conditioned buildings, but the whole point of camping is to be outdoors, so we were outside quite a lot. Carrying around water bottles wasn't in vogue then, so we had to make sure the staff and the campers drank plenty of water. Of course, you could carry a trusty old canteen (usually the Army surplus kind) strapped to your hip.

Part of the weekly routine for the staff members was to spend a day off at Walt Disney World, which had opened less than a year earlier. Only the Magic Kingdom was there then. Orlando was about an hour away, so groups of staff would drive down early in the morning, stay until the theme park closed and drive back in the middle of the night. Central Florida was not yet the theme park capital of the world and Disney was really a novel experience for all of us. Most of the staff had those mouse ear hats with their names embroidered on them.

It is quite an experience to create something new. We named the roads, the camp sites and started creating the traditions that every camp develops over time.

To my surprise and disappointment, in 2004 the camp property was sold. The council could no longer afford to operate it because of cutbacks in United Way funding.[8] I regret it tremendously. But that summer was probably the high point of my professional Scouting career, and one of the high points of my life. When I think back on it, I realize it was one of the most pleasurable I could imagine. As hard as it was, I left there feeling a sense of real accomplishment. If I could have been a camp director for a living, I might have stayed in that line of work. Fortunately, the main camp area was leased in 2006 by the Gulf Ridge Council, BSA, headquartered in Tampa, which allows troops to do rustic camping on the property.

I took another District Executive position in Orlando in early 1973 in hopes I might find it more enjoyable than South Florida, which even then, was becoming very complicated to live in and make Scouting work.

I didn't find what I was looking for in Central Florida Council either, though. The pressure, the hours and the relatively low pay finally got to me. My bosses and I were not getting along and they told me there was no more job for me there in June of 1975. Rather than find a job in another council, I decided to look for different work. I finally ended up selling real estate and supervising building construction, which led me apply to a couple of law schools, hoping to become a real estate lawyer. By September of 1977, I was at Florida State University College of Law. I never left Scouting, though. I have been continuously registered in some capacity ever since.

Chapter Two

Boy Scouting

The Beginnings of Boy Scouting
A Worldwide Event

A short explanation of the origins and meaning of Scouting is in order. Robert Baden-Powell was a 19th Century British military officer who was dissatisfied with the training his men were receiving.[9] He felt they were not being taught to care for themselves when they were on their own and could not assume leadership if their officers and sergeants were not with them. During the Boer War, around the end of the 19th Century, his force was surrounded and besieged at a little town in South Africa called Mafeking.

As a result of the siege, where he held out for 217 days in the face of vastly superior numbers until relieved, he became a huge military hero in Britain and was made the youngest general officer in the army. This sudden fame made it possible for him to get published a small book, *Aids to Scouting*.[10] This book was a summary of a series of lectures on the subject of military scouting and laid out training exercises for tracking, observation, woodcraft and other useful skills for soldiers in the field. At some point he discovered that many British boys were buying and reading this book.

Like many other British men, Baden-Powell was concerned about the state of youth in the country. With encouragement from others he ultimately wrote the book *Scouting for Boys*, laying out a similar set of games for boys to use in becoming "scouts," as the word is used in the military sense, tracking and observing, as well as taking care of themselves on their own.[11] As a result of the book, and B-P's fame, boys all over the United Kingdom were reading the book and forming "Scout patrols." Sometimes they recruited men to be their "Scoutmaster."

Before long an organization was born. B-P, as he was popularly known, had thought the program would be useful to boys' organizations already in existence, like the YMCA, but he soon saw that wasn't the way it would play out. So he formed the British Scouts Association and became the Founder of Scouting in the world. He was not a particularly wealthy man by standards of the time, but he never was paid a salary for his efforts.

Baden-Powell saw Scouting as a game for boys, played under the tutelage of men. In it, boys would wear a uniform that identified them, with badges that showed their achievements. He wanted to see boys become physically fit and be able to take care of themselves in the outdoors. But he wanted something else, too. He wanted to see them develop character and become good citizens. Some have thought he wanted to see them become soldiers of the King and help build the British Empire, but his writings and public speeches show that this was not his intent.[12]

As part of later editions of Scouting for Boys, B-P included The Scout Promise and the Scout Law. They read as follows:

The Scout Promise

On my honour I promise that I will do my best–
To do my duty to God and the King,
To help other people at all times,
To obey the Scout Law.

The Scout Law

1. A Scout's honour is to be trusted.
2. A Scout is loyal to the King, his country, his Scouters, his parents, his employers and to those under him.
3. A Scout's duty is to be useful and help others.
4. A Scout is a friend to all, and a brother to every other Scout, no matter to what country, class or creed the other may belong.
5. A Scout is courteous.
6. A Scout is a friend to animals.
7. A Scout obeys the orders of his parents, Patrol Leader, or Scoutmaster without question.
8. A Scout smiles and whistles under all difficulties.
9. A Scout is thrifty.
10. A Scout is clean in thought, word, and deed.[13]

It probably comes as a revelation to the average person that Baden-Powell really created a game that was designed to appeal to boys who were looking for fun and adventure and teach them citizenship, character and physical fitness. Those objectives and those alone, are the rationale behind the Scouting movement. The rest of the program is intended to capture their interest and keep them involved.

It worked on a scale that few other movements have worked before. It very quickly spread, literally, around the world. Of course, the "sun never set on the British Empire," so that, in itself, ensured a widespread growth. But other countries quickly adopted Scouting. One of those was destined to become the biggest stronghold of Scouting anywhere: the United States of America.

Baden-Powell soon retired from the Army, reportedly on the advice of King Edward VII, who suggested he could better serve his country by promoting Scouting. At the outbreak of World War

One, he placed himself at the disposal of the War Office. Lord Kitchener never gave him any duties, however, reportedly saying he could find numerous able generals, but no one could be found who could carry on the invaluable work of the Boy Scouts.

The Boy Men

This is a good point to digress a little into what is a phenomenon that is hard to describe, but is easily observed. Some men (many women would say all men) never really lose their boyish nature. They mostly learn to bury it under layers of education, professionalism and societal expectations, but when they have an opportunity to relate to a bunch of youngsters, this side of their nature shows up. These are what Baden-Powell called "boy-men." B-P said, "The Scoutmaster teaches boys to play the game by doing so himself."[14]

Professional Scouters generally don't have to worry about this aspect of their personality, because they seldom work directly with boys. Most professionals obviously are concerned about boys or they wouldn't be in the business they are in, but they don't usually need to interact directly with them. Volunteers in the Boy Scout troop do. The extent to which they are able to really connect with boys has a lot to do with the success or failure of the troop program. I have never seen a large Scout troop that didn't have a leader the boys all adore.

I know that some Scoutmasters could lead a bunch of adolescent and preadolescent boys into a blazing inferno while others have trouble getting them excited about going for pizza.

You can watch boys at a Scout meeting and pretty much tell how they feel about their leaders just by the way they act toward them. What you won't see is how the boys act when there isn't anyone else around. If they like their leader, they will tease him, call him by nicknames and sometimes play tricks on him. This doesn't mean any lack of respect and it usually will not happen when outsiders are present.

There is a great autobiographical book, long out of print, by Rice E. Cochran, who wrote the screenplay for the movie, *Mr. Scoutmaster*, starring Clifton Webb, called *Be Prepared*, that does a great job of describing a boy-man (Cochran) in action.[15]

B-P also said something to the effect that boys could find adventure in a dirty old duck pond and, if their leader was a boy-man, he could see it, too.

Boy Scouting in the U.S.A.

The history of the Boy Scouts of America is a huge American epic.

In the early 20th Century in the U.S., urbanization was at level never before seen in this country and its effects were beginning to be seen in American youth. Juvenile delinquency was on the rise and the youth were not as physically fit as they had been when most lived on farms.

Urban American boys had relatively a lot of free time. Where farm boys had worked from dawn to dusk, city boys had less work to do. They had been removed from the outdoors and there was as yet no mass media to occupy their time. They were ready for an organization which was theirs alone, to give them something designed for boys to do.

The idea of Scouting, with its uniforms, badges and activities along with other boys, was exactly the thing. They soon even had their own magazine, *Boys' Life*, which came to them in the mail and was written for them. The fact that Scouting started from "the ground up," with boys starting their own patrols and troops, shows just how ready they were.

Organizations like the YMCA and Big Brothers were on the rise. Social workers everywhere were concerned. Famous men like Daniel Carter Beard and Ernest Thompson Seton had both created popular organizations that sought to improve boys physically and morally by bringing them closer to the outdoors.[16]

So, the men who began Scouting as an organization in the U.S. were acting on an idea whose time had come. A reading of history shows that timing is everything. If Germany had not gotten what they perceived as a raw deal in World War I and then suffered economic collapse, Hitler might never have come to power.

At any other time in history the idea might not have worked. But, in 1910 everything was in place for Scouting to take off in the United States. Men and boys were in the right place at the right time and Baden-Powell, along with Seton and Beard, had given them the right mechanism.

In researching this book, I have read a great many council histories. While there are great similarities, there are so many unique stories that it would take another book to encompass them. An example of similarities among council histories is the frequency with which the "Good Turn" story appears.

The slogan of both the British and the American Scout organizations is "Do a Good Turn Daily," which means doing an unsolicited act of assistance to some person or animal needing help during each day. It was, in fact, a good turn that resulted in the start of Boy Scouting as an organization in the U.S.

Once Scouting got a foothold in the U.S., young boys began actively looking for good turns, which they generally call "good deeds," to do. Sometimes they really did help little old ladies cross the street, but they also carried groceries for people or held babies while a mother transacted some business. Some of the recipients of these good turns were wealthy, influential people. They must have thought that any organization that could get scruffy little boys to voluntarily help others must have something going for it. These people frequently contributed money, property, civic influence and other things needed to establish a Scout organization in their area.

The Creation of a Profession

At the beginning of an early Scouting personnel handbook, the author quotes from James Truslow Adams' *Epic of America,*

> If the American dream is to come true and to abide with us, it will, at bottom, depend on the people themselves. We cannot become a great democracy by giving ourselves up as individuals to selfishness, physical comfort, and cheap amusements. The very foundation of the American dream of a better and richer life for all is, that all, in varying degrees, shall be capable of wanting to share in it.

> If we are to make the dream come true we must all work together, no longer to build bigger, but to build better.

> The American dream–the means provided by the accumulated resources of the people themselves, a public intelligent enough to use them, and men of high distinction, themselves a part of the great democracy, devoting themselves to the good of the whole, uncloistered.[17]

> Scouting seeks to make the American dream come true for the youth it serves.[18]

This isn't meant to be a history of the start of Boy Scouting in the U.S.A., but we have to talk about it a little to give the reader a background for the stories of the men that the book is about. There are lots of books about the history of Scouting, and some of them are listed in the Bibliography. Scouting started in Britain in 1907.

Many in the U.S. were concerned about the moral and physical state of its youth, just as in Britain. Some Americans, like author and naturalist Ernest Thompson Seton and Daniel Carter Beard, an author and social reformer, had already started organizations for boys to get them in the outdoors. Scouting in the U.S. really got started when Chicago businessman William D. Boyce encountered a young man on a London street. The story varies as to whether Boyce was lost in a London fog or just needed help crossing the street, since traffic was coming from the wrong direction, but the story is that the boy took Boyce to his destination and refused a tip, saying he was a Scout and that a part of his obligation was to do a "good turn" to someone every day. The original good turn in American Scouting. Even that story may not be true. Some Scouting scholars believe that Boyce, a promoter, just used it to give an added boost to the legend of the start of Scouting. What is certain is that Boyce, who could scarcely have been unaware of British Scouting, visited Scout headquarters in London and got information and a Scout handbook to bring home. He also determined that the best way for Scouting to get a foothold in the U.S. was as a separate, American, organization.

When Boyce returned and founded a corporation named the Boy Scouts of America, it attracted attention. Other civic minded Americans, including Beard and Seton, also established contact with the British Scouts. Seton was in contact with Baden-Powell before the beginning of the formal movement in

Britain. Through amalgamation of various groups and the backing of civic organizations, described more fully in the next section, by 1910 the Boy Scouts of America had been incorporated with headquarters in New York City. There were just a couple of men in that office. All over the country, though, men and boys were getting together and starting Boy Scout troops. Sometimes it was the men who initiated it and sometimes it was the boys.

The first American Scout handbook, *Handbook for Boys*, was in print by 1911.[19] Boys got hold of the books and wanted to start Scout patrols and troops. In the beginning, Scoutmasters got their "commissions" from New York and had to deal with that office to get badges, uniforms, and other things necessary to run Scout troops. In 1913, a handbook was written for Scoutmasters.[20]

As is the case with most not-for-profit corporations, the BSA was started by a group of well-meaning men of means who obtained the necessary community support, funding and legal work to get the organization going. Of course, these men did not have the time in most cases to devote to the day-to-day operation of Scouting.

In Britain, Baden-Powell had been obliged to give up his military duties, where he was a Lieutenant General serving as Inspector General of the British Army, and spend the rest of his life working to promote Scouting around the world. In the United States, a young Washington, DC, attorney, James E. West, was retained as permanent Executive Secretary in 1911, a title which soon became Chief Scout Executive. This system was followed in naming other professional employees as the organization expanded and the professionals became known as Scout Executives.[21]

There were of course internal power struggles in the early days. The men who joined together to found the BSA were powerful and influential men in their own right.

Ernest Thompson Seton, perhaps best known for the book *Wild Animals I Have Known,* with the story of Lobo the wolf, had created his own boys organization, the Woodcraft Indians.[22] Daniel Carter "Uncle Dan" Beard was another man who started a boys' movement, Sons of Daniel Boone, which later became the Boy Pioneers, and had a great youth following. Seton was using the Native American as a theme for his groups. Seton saw them as noble savages whereas Beard looked at American Indians as a bad example and founded his group on the activities of the American frontiersman, including scouting.

There was disagreement about how exactly the program was to be carried out. Generally, the British system was followed, but some British customs and traditions were discarded by the Americans. There was much discussion about how to phrase the American Scout Oath and Law, particularly when it came to inclusion of religious beliefs. The British Laws did not include "A Scout Is Reverent," which became the twelfth of the American Scout Laws.[23]

Seton, who was Chief Scout and had written *Handbook for Boys,* had some very definite ideas about how the BSA should be run, which ran counter to what James E. West had in mind. As a result of their inability to reach a compromise, Seton dropped out of Scouting. Most of the rest stayed on though to create the organization which has evolved into one of the largest youth movements in history, with the largest Scouting membership of any country in the world.

Both Seton and Beard felt that they were the rightful founders of the Scouting movement. Beard remained with the BSA until his death, but was always a thorn in West's side over one thing or another.

Seton, in particular, felt that Baden-Powell owed a lot of his program to Seton's ideas as taken from their early correspondence. There is no question that some of Baden-Powell's Scouting principles are taken from Seton's work. It is also true that many of the games, advancement programs and the Scout Oath as set forth in *Scouting for Boys* were very similar to those of Seton as set out in his *Birch Bark Roll*, which B-P had access to prior to writing his book. Although it is almost certain that Seton would never have been able to found a movement on the order of Scouting, and arguments can be made that he should have received more credit from Baden-Powell and the BSA, Seton died believing he was the creator of Scouting.[24] Great men, unfortunately, can have big egos no matter how well-intentioned their causes.

Both Seton and Beard also were aggrieved that, when the highest award of the Boy Scouts of America, the Silver Buffalo, was created and bestowed, they were not among the very first recipients.[25]

Right up to the present day, there have been many critics of professional Scouting. In Britain and most other countries, Scouting programs have small professional staffs and everything else is run by volunteers in their spare time.

The difficulty in 1910 was that the United States is much larger geographically than most of those countries and did not have a class of nobility like the British and the Russians did at the time (Russia had Scouting up until the revolution of 1917 and started it up again after the fall of the Soviet Union) who had no real jobs, plenty of money and could devote their time and energy to traveling around setting up Scouting.

One drawback of a large professional staff, as with government programs, is that people are willing to stand back and let the pros do the work. And, like the bureaucrats who run a national or local government, the professionals come to regard Scouting to some degree as "their" program and the volunteers as foot soldiers.

In theory, the local council executive boards run the council as in any corporation and supervise hiring and firing of professionals, but in reality they tend to rely on the guidance and direction of the professionals, sometimes to the detriment of the program. The other problem is that you must pay these people a livable wage and provide them with office space, telephones, computers, vehicles and some kind of expense account. Nowadays that takes a great deal of money. Although the professionals are trained to raise money, they spend a lot of time at it. As a result, volunteers sometimes wonder what it is exactly that the professionals are doing for *them*.

It is also true that, at least in one case, the professional leadership of the BSA almost took the movement off the tracks. I refer to this elsewhere in the saga of Boypower '76, the 1967-1976 effort to make one boy out every three in America a Scout by setting goals that councils could not possibly meet. Although most councils escaped the fate of the thirteen that were caught red-handed creating "paper" units out of thin air, no council that I am aware of was untouched by the problem. Virtually every professional Scouter during those years was forced to either cheat, walk a very fine line in doing things that bordered on unethical or look the other way in the knowledge that others were doing this.

Professionals, as dedicated as they are, are in the business of Scouting. And make no mistake, it is a business. It cannot work any other way. Once a man's or woman's livelihood becomes tied to this or any movement, from that moment forward they must be beholden to whatever goals and means are set by management or they must resign and find another means of making a living. Still, I cannot imagine that American Scouting could have grown to the size and have the impact that it has had for over one hundred years without the efforts of a sizeable professional staff.

From the beginning, Scout Executives looked upon themselves as members of a fraternity. There was a publication, called *The Scout Executive*, which was going out monthly to professionals by 1922.[26]

There was also a death benefit plan. Called the Scout Executives Insurance Alliance, professionals could enroll and upon the death of any member of the alliance, each member would be assessed a set amount to pay a death benefit to his widow. In the case of an early death of a member, his widow received $500 in two days (apparently, some reserves were kept on hand), and a total of $1515.00 was given to her within thirty days. This was in a time when a thousand dollars a year would be a handsome salary for anyone in social work or teaching.[27]

In 1936, at a conference for Scout Executives, the Scouters were asked to explain why they continued to serve in the profession. Here are the answers:

1. "In order to contribute to enrichment of boys' lives and thus serve my community, my country, and my Creator."

2. "Because of personal satisfaction which comes from service."

3. "To improve myself in terms of avocations in order that I may be a better citizen."

4. "To be recognized as one who serves in a worthwhile cause."[28]

Those would be worthy rewards for anyone in a career.

Before long, the operation had become unwieldy. There were too many Scout troops widely spread over the U.S. and its territories for everything to be done from a central office. That's how it was done in the U.K., and largely still is. The U.S. is a much vaster country than Britain, however, and, in the early 20th Century, more diverse. In 1912, Sir Robert Baden-Powell, who, by then, had been knighted by King Edward VII, came to the U.S. and toured the country along with Chief Scout Executive, Dr. West.

During that tour, West realized that some kind of regional distribution was going to have to be set up.[29] Around 1920, the BSA created twelve Regions and set up an office in each of them, staffed with a Regional Executive and several deputies.[30]

Part of the job of these offices would be to assist citizens in localities where they had the resources and the desire to create a local organization, called a council, that could then hire "[A] high-class man who will give his entire time as a Scout Executive to the development of the movement, not to be the Scoutmaster of our boys, but to train [other qualified men] to be the Scoutmasters . . . to teach churches and schools the value of the Scout program and how to use it."[31]

Local councils, like the national one, were corporations formed by groups of citizens who then hired men to be the Scout Executives. It should be noted that the National Council issues charters to local councils and that these charters can be revoked if the council does not follow national guidelines, including hiring an approved Scout Executive. All important decisions are made by the executive board of the national or the local council, but of course great weight is given to the experience of the professionals. The professionals are generally the ones who draft the agendas for the volunteer boards to make decisions upon. It would be wrong to say that the running of the BSA at the national and local level is entirely in the hands of the professionals, but in current practice it's not far from the truth.

Thus began Scouting as a profession. The ranks of these men would soon grow from a few dozen to several thousand. Today, there are about 7,000 men and women professionals in the BSA.[32]

Early councils were divided into two classes: class one councils, those who had a Scout Executive, and class two councils, those who didn't, and were overseen by a volunteer, the Scout Commissioner.

According to the 1913 *Handbook for Scout Masters* [sic]: "A budget of $2000 or more a year will enable any city to set up an effective organization and employ a Scout Executive."[33] The book went on to say, "[T]he employment of such a man has been found absolutely necessary in the larger cities of the country, in order to carry on the work of the district with efficiency and despatch [sic]."[34]

When the twelve Regions were created, the chief of the region was called Regional Scout Executive and as local councils began to be formed, the top hired man was called Scout Executive. Most councils were founded under the leadership of a volunteer, called a Commissioner, until they could afford to hire a full-time man. Later there were Assistant Scout Executives, Field Directors and District Scout Executives. Today, there are even more titles, as the program has expanded and evolved.

Recruiting of men to the profession was, and still is, an ongoing and important job. In the earliest days, men came from other programs for boys, often with no real background in Scouting. Most of them had been involved in what was at the time called "boys' work." Many, as will be seen, came from the ranks of the YMCA.

As time went on, of course, men who had been Scouts as boys, worked on camp staffs and served as troop leaders began to be recruited. Some just couldn't imagine doing anything else. As time went on, some Scout Executives earned a reputation as recruiters. One such was A.C. Gaskin, Scout Executive of Lake Charles, Louisiana. Gaskin put his entire council volunteer staff, from council president on down, on the team. They were given the guidelines as to what kind of men were being sought and told to cultivate such men whenever they were found.[35]

Southeast Region Conference, 1970

This is a story of a relatively modern conference of Scout Executives, and it illustrates the kind of fraternalism that has always existed among professional Scouters.

A new Region, the Southeast Region had been created and the first Regional Conference was to be held at the Doral Resort in Miami. It was a major occasion, an opportunity to meet old friends from all over as well as the top brass of the new Region. Spurgeon Gaskin, whose story will be told, was the new Regional Executive.

The conference itself consisted of seminars and meetings about Scouting, quite a bit of it having to do with the new Boypower '76 agenda, which turned into such a disaster. But, there was plenty of time for recreational activities and I got to play my first round of golf on the course at the Doral. I played a lot more after that, usually somewhat better. Golf is a good way to meet and cultivate volunteers at the upper levels in Scouting.

At that time, a great contest was going on between the Atlanta Council and ours in Miami, as to who would end the year with the most membership and units in the Region. We wore buttons, saying "Beat Atlanta," and there was a friendly rivalry underway. We younger professionals were always looking for something exciting to do. One night we got the idea of getting a coffin and holding a mock funeral for Atlanta. Since we were on home turf, we eventually found a volunteer with connections to get us an appropriate casket. The next night, we arranged to have this "funeral" in the interim between two speeches from the podium. Unknown to us, the powers had decided to insert a eulogy for professional Scouters recently deceased at this exact point. In we came, carrying our coffin, just as the crowd was bowing in prayer for the dead Scouters. Needless to say, we beat a hasty retreat and rescheduled our ceremony.

The conference served its purpose. We went away, refreshed and re-invigorated for the job ahead. We had compared notes with our friends from other councils and gotten ideas we could use in our own.

Schiff Scout Reservation
A National Training School

There had been training for Scout Executives and biennial conferences in 1920, 1922 and 1924. During the conferences, training was part of the agenda for all in attendance. The men heard lectures from experts in business, religion, finance, social work and others who had valuable input for the business of Boy Scouting. In 1922, for example, they were told how what they were doing was selling. They needed to do all the things salesmen do: prospecting, selling themselves on their product and their territory, scheduling their time and closing.[36] The features were not all that different from the 1970 conference in Miami.

The National Training School was established in 1925, the first session being held at Bear Mountain Inn in New York State in the fall of that year. Forty-three men attended the four week course. An additional thirty-four classes were held between

October 1925 and September 1933, at locations mainly around New York City. Almost 1100 men got training. In 1932, the BSA acquired a 500 acre site in central New Jersey.

The dedication to Mortimer L. Schiff, a prominent national volunteer from a wealthy family who had recently died, was most impressive. It was attended by the governor of the state and featured reading of a letter from President Roosevelt.

Schiff Scout Reservation, as it was known, became the home of professional Scouter training from then until it was sold by the BSA in 1979. It was also the scene of many historical gatherings of Boy Scouts and Scouters over the years. To see it disestablished was a blow to all of those who knew and loved it. It was deemed necessary because the value of the land had become astronomical, the national headquarters of BSA was being moved to the Dallas, Texas, area, a more central location in the country, and the training program for Scout Executives was being revamped once again to bring it more in line with modern Scouting.

Chapter Three

The Founding of the B.S.A.

James E. West was the first Chief Scout Executive of the BSA. However, he wasn't the first American professional Scouter. That honor belongs to a Canadian-born YMCA executive named Edgar M. Robinson. At the time of the founding of the BSA, Robinson had been a YMCA camp director for 20 years, and was aware of Scouting in Britain and its infant units in the U.S. When William D. Boyce incorporated the Boy Scouts of America in Chicago in 1910, Robinson went to see the businessman and was able to convince Boyce to allow him to set up a national committee for the BSA and to take over title of the corporation. Boyce had no interest in actually leading the BSA and funded Robinson to the tune of $1,000 a month to help get started.

It was Robinson who opened the first national office next door to the YMCA facility he occupied in New York City. He staffed it with another YMCA worker and a stenographer, who soon had to deal with lots of letters from boys and men who wanted to know how to start Scout troops. Robinson also brought Ernest Thompson Seton and other men who were planning to start Scouting organizations on their own into the fledgling movement.

It was then necessary to get together a group of men from existing organizations for boys and put together the first BSA National Committee with Ernest Thompson Seton as chairman.

The first U.S. Scout camp soon followed, at Silver Bay in upstate New York, almost by accident. The encampment had been arranged much earlier for men involved in boys' work and the boys from their programs, but all the camp leaders were by then in the thrall of Scouting, so it became an unofficial Boy Scout camp with Seton and others teaching Scouting skills during a two-week event. This "first encampment," as it has been called, was an experiment in the development of the American Boy Scout program. Ernest Thompson Seton, for example, may have designed the first Boy Scout uniform during the camp.[37] What followed was a major growth of Scouting all over the country.

In pictures, Robinson looked like a rather stuffy schoolteacher, and thought of himself as not the kind of man that boys would be attracted to as a leader.

According to some who knew him at the time, he was actually a very pleasant man and enjoyed the outdoors where he could be informal and let his hair down. Seton and Beard were charismatic men who had no difficulty in getting flocks of boys to sit at their feet for hours and are certainly better remembered than Robinson, but it was he, with the background and resources of the YMCA at his disposal, who brought about the establishment of the BSA as a major player in youth development.[38] Robinson remained closely associated with Scouting in an unofficial capacity until his retirement from the YMCA.

Edgar M. Robinson never had any intention of leaving the YMCA, so his major contribution to the BSA was his recruitment of the next and permanent executive secretary, Washington DC attorney James E. West.

West took over and shortly his title was changed to Chief Scout Executive. It was West and the other men who succeeded in getting Congress to charter the BSA, which added great prestige to the whole endeavor. Robinson remained with the YMCA until his retirement in 1927 and died in 1951 as a mere footnote in the history of the BSA.

Chapter Four

William D. Boyce and Lone Scouting

William D. Boyce was the man who really brought Scouting to America, through his supposed meeting with a still-unknown British Scout. Although Boyce disappeared early in the history of the BSA, he made a contribution to the movement that lasted to the present day.[39]

Boyce was a publisher and made his money by selling magazines. A major part of his sales force was young boys. His magazines would be shipped across the country to boys who would distribute them to customers to whom they had sold subscriptions.

It occurred to Boyce that, since many boys lived on remote farms in areas where no Scout troops existed, it would be possible to create a program for them that they could do on their own, with the help of his magazine. Boyce incorporated the Lone Scouts of America.

Boys were given ceremonies to perform for joining and tasks to master in order to earn badges that could be purchased from Boyce. He also enrolled all his young magazine agents as Lone Scouts. The membership swelled to 50,000.

He found a wide reception for the magazine, which could be mailed to any place that had Rural Free Delivery (RFD), which by this time was almost everywhere that had a road. Boys joined and participated in this program of which the magazine was a major part. Portions of the magazine were written by boys.

Boyce's part in the venture came to a conclusion in 1924, when it merged with the BSA. It still survives today so that any boy, no matter how remote, can be a part of Scouting.

When Lone Scouting became part of the BSA, John P. Wallace was appointed to chair the Department of Rural Scouting. He apparently was never a paid professional. He published a magazine, *Wallace's Farmer.* There was already a rural Scouting program in the BSA, which was reaching out to farm boys too isolated to be part of a Troop.

The Lone Scout program was gradually modified and adapted to merge into the BSA program. Since most boys in the United States lived in rural areas in the Twenties and Thirties, this represented a significant recruiting opportunity for the BSA, if it could get past the parental concerns about how much time their boys would spend away from duties on the farm and how they would get to and from any meetings they had to go to.

Wallace got to work with 4-H and other organizations working with farm folks and established some merit badges that were aimed at rural boys. Wallace was active at state fairs and other farm venues to promote Scouting. He received the Silver Buffalo in 1938.[40]

Chapter Five

James E. West, Chief Scout Executive, Builder of a Movement

It would be almost impossible to overstate the impact that Dr. James E. West (the doctorate was an honorary LLD, but people generally called him by the title) had on the Boy Scouts America, from his first day on the job in 1911 right down to the present day.

No man, not even Lord Baden-Powell himself, had as much influence on the BSA as Dr. West. He was complex, dictatorial and bureaucratic. He was described as "prickly."[41] As a result, apparently, few people really liked him personally. In fact, most of the professionals feared him. A characteristic anecdote was recorded from the 1937 Boy Scout National Jamboree.

The Jamboree was held in Washington DC, in the area of the Mall, west of the Washington Monument and across the Potomac on the site where the Pentagon stands today. Entrance and exit were strictly controlled and boys could not easily leave the site. Leaders could come and go, but there was a curfew in effect.

An Eagle Scout from New Mexico, J. Herbert Priddy, was attending as a leader with the Jamboree Troop from his council and one evening he left the camp to visit some friends in Washington. When he returned, he was late, and he was stopped at the entrance and taken to headquarters, where he was ushered into the presence of West. Although Priddy explained that he was late because of his visit, Dr. West removed the Eagle badge from the young man's shirt. West told him that he had violated the first Scout Law, "A Scout is Trustworthy," which went on to specify that, "If [a Scout] were to violate his honor by not doing exactly a given task when trusted on his honor, he may be directed to hand over his Scout Badge."[42]

According to West, Priddy had violated this Law by failing to give leadership to his Jamboree troop. West, of course, was a lawyer and probably knew in his heart that this was a pretty legalistic (not to mention petty) interpretation of that point of the Law, but at the time, it was he who set down what the Scout Law meant.

Priddy went back to his campsite, divested of his proudest possession and spent the rest of the Jamboree without it. On the last day, West summoned him once again and inquired as to whether Priddy had learned the lesson. On being assured that he had, West returned the badge to him. The young man went on to become a Scoutmaster and principal of a junior high school, so it can be assumed that he took the lesson to heart.[43] However, the incident appears to be typical of the kind of micro management to which West was addicted. This was a man who once, when asked to inspect a troop in New York, asked a staff member in the National Office to show him how to tie a few Scout knots so that he could demonstrate them to the boys.

West grew up under the worst kind of circumstances. Orphaned at an early age and spent his formative years in an institution that sounds like something out of the story of Oliver Twist. He developed tuberculosis which settled in his hip and leg, and ended up with a leg that was inches shorter than the other. He used crutches to get around. Although he got rid of the crutches eventually, he wore a brace and walked with a cane all of his life and apparently was in pain a good deal of the time. The cane was sometimes used to sweep everything off a desktop in the National Office if he thought it too cluttered and once to knock out a train window that the porter failed to open for him.

West never camped in his life and it was a source of great resentment to both Seton and Beard that he was neither an outdoorsman nor a "boy-man". People feared him and executives were reluctant to speak counter to any of his ideas.

West was, however, exactly what was needed to establish the Boy Scouts of America as one of the largest youth organizations in the world with a total membership larger than that of Scouting in all other countries combined well before mid-century.

As has been mentioned, the BSA is unlike most other countries in having most of its power concentrated in the hands of the professionals. It was Dr. James E. West who made it so. Early on, he made the statement, "The function of the Volunteer is not to dominate over the Executive, for he, the Executive is essential. There must be a head who is responsible . . . [but] we must not in our success lose sight of the fact that we always have been, and increasingly, we are always going to be dependent upon the place that the man of affairs, the man of active business and educational connections has with the Boy Scout Movement."[44] Then and today, council presidents and members of executive boards are men and women of wealth and power, people who can raise money and influence community affairs.

In 1921, the first manual was written for professional Scouters. It has no named author, but West's philosophy was very clear in it:

> Scouting is a profession for the Scout Executive, because of the vital social quality of the work of serving the

community, through the art of character building, companionship, and leadership of its boyhood.

No man merits consideration who does not have a positive religious tone and recognizedly [sic] high moral quality on which the other needed qualities of leadership are to be builded. [sic] Only he can hope to train a child in the way to go who goes that way himself. The moral quality of the profession is therefore basic and imperative.

This is not a manual about building fires or pitching tents. Professional Scouters were not outdoorsmen, they were recruiters and managers. Indeed, West cautions them against being leaders of boys.

Surely he must not have personal relations to individual boys by which he gives them a special service or special privileges. There is a practice, among some executives, fortunately true of the very few . . . It is not a proper relation It is too personal, too intimate, too discriminating. It is not wise. We cannot be too emphatic on this point.[45]

Read today, those words may take on a meaning not intended by its author. West wasn't considering the possibility of executives having improper relationships with boys. What he wanted to avoid was the kind of personal attraction to boys that was part of the makeup of men like Uncle Dan Beard or Ernest Thompson Seton. West was not such a man himself and he sought to mold the profession in his own image. Of course, as will be seen in individual stories of professionals, it didn't work very well, because in the 1920s and today, men will be in Scouting and in professional Scouting because they are boy-men and because boys are always looking for strong male leaders that they can admire and be friends with. Until the late Sixties, almost every professional had grown up a Scout, worked at summer camps and Scout troops. Many still come from a Scouting background today. They just naturally relate well to boys.

Some people did have concerns about the numbers of professionals in Scouting in the U.S. and the business-like methods West used to organize them. One of them was Baden-Powell. The Founder simply did not recognize the differences in the culture of the United States as opposed to that of Britain. As mentioned, this country had no aristocracy or even a significant number of men who retired in their forties and fifties as well-off British men sought to do. Even wealthy Americans do not usually retire until they are well on in years. West once complained that the Founder had "yet to make one single reference to his appreciation of the part I have had and now have in the Boy Scout Movement here in America; in fact his attitude has been that of regarding us here–as the other executives with whom he comes in contact–as so many 'hired men' . . . "[46]

Dr. West reigned over the BSA until 1943. No Chief Scout Executive since has been allowed to remain at the helm so long. After West, no one would want them to. In the 21st Century, change simply comes too rapidly to have a man at the helm for too long, however good his ideas may be.

James E. West didn't want to retire and continued to come up with reasons why he should not. The organization had a mandatory retirement age of 65 then, but West thought the organization couldn't go on without him. Finally, the BSA President and Board simply were adamant and West agreed to retire.

However, he got quite a retirement package, including an annual pension of $20,000 and the permanent title of Chief Scout. The professional service was so beholden to West that, in order to replace him it was necessary to go outside the ranks of executives for his successor.

No other Executive, except possibly the late Alden G. Barber–it was he who oversaw Boypower '76–has had anything like the impact on Scouting that West did.

West was pretty much isolated from the organization after his retirement. He was not invited to speak at major occasions, his picture never appeared in the organization's magazine and he was not asked to actually do anything as Chief Scout. His health went downhill from his tuberculosis and Addison's disease, and he was eventually bedridden until his death in 1948.

Today, his grave site is not well known and his marker has the British fleur-di-lis instead of the BSA trefoil and eagle. It is probable that more Scouters and Scouts from the U.S. visit the grave of Lord Baden-Powell, which is in Nyeri, Kenya, than West's in Valhalla, NY.

Only recently has West been "rehabilitated," in that a fellowship was created in his name for donors of a minimum of $1000 to Scouting.

Chapter Six

The Chief Scout Executives

These are the eleven men who have served as Chief Scout Executive since James E. West:

Elbert K. Fretwell, PhD., 1943-1948
Arthur A. Schuck, 1948-1960
Joseph A. Brunton, Jr., 1960-1966
Alden G. Barber, 1967-1976
Harvey L. Price, 1976-1979
James Lee Tarr, 1979-1984
Ben H. Love, 1984-1993
Jere B. Ratcliff, 1993-2000
Roy L. Williams, 2000-2007
Robert J. Mazzuca, 2007-2012
Wayne Brock, 2012-

Only one of these men did not come from the ranks of professional Scouters. Dr. Fretwell, who was Dean of the Teachers' college at Columbia University and had long been involved in Scouting at the national level, was selected, as mentioned above, because he was not one of James E. West's men, and, apparently, his five years at the helm was enough to counteract West's autocratic policies at the national office.[47]

Arthur A. Schuck

Arthur A. Schuck was the third Chief Scout Executive of the BSA. He served during the period of continuing transition from the James E. West methods through postwar America, into the year of the Fiftieth Anniversary celebration of the BSA. His tenure in office lasted twelve years, but his professional career spanned forty-one of the very early years of Scouting in the U.S.

Born in 1895, Schuck graduated from high school and took extension correspondence courses, but apparently did not earn a college degree. He first entered "boys' work" in Newark, New Jersey, and then went to work for the BSA in 1917. He had been a volunteer Scouter prior to that time as a Scoutmaster and a Deputy Scout Commissioner.

He served as a professional in Lancaster, Pennsylvania, before founding the Chester County Council in Chester County, Pennsylvania. Between 1919 and 1922, Schuck was Scout Executive of the Daniel Boone Council in Reading, Pennsylvania and then served as Regional Executive of what would become Region Three.

He then went to the National Office of the BSA to work in finance and organization. In 1931, he became Director of Operations, a job he held until becoming Deputy Chief Scout Executive in 1943.

After James E. West retired, Schuck became the Scout Executive in Los Angeles, California, then and now one of the nation's largest councils.

In 1948, Schuck was selected to become Chief Scout Executive of the BSA. He served as Chief during a time of quiet national transition. Harry Truman and Dwight Eisenhower were Presidents of the United States and the year he retired, 1960, was the year of the election of John F. Kennedy. While he made no radical changes in the BSA, there were many subtle changes in the movement. The world saw the Berlin Blockade, which confirmed the beginning of the Cold War; the Korean War, which made us really anxious about Communist aggression; and Sputnik, the first man-made satellite to orbit the earth, launched by the Soviets, which began the Space Age. However, Schuck saw that the purpose of the BSA was what it always has been, "To give to America a new generation of men of character, with ingrained qualities that make for good citizenship."[48]

His service was recognized not only the U.S., but in several foreign countries. He received the BSA's Silver Buffalo award and the Bronze Wolf of the World Scouting Organization. Schuck also was the recipient of a number of honorary doctoral degrees. Schuck retired as Chief Scout Executive in 1960 and passed away in February, 1963.[49] He was the last Chief to be addressed as "Doctor" and also the last to receive the Silver Buffalo while in office.

Joseph A. Brunton, Jr.

Joseph A. Brunton Jr. was selected to become the fourth Chief, following Dr. Schuck, when he retired in 1960. Brunton was the first Chief Scout Executive I ever saw in person, much less met, which I did when he came to Philmont Scout Ranch in 1965 to inspect the damage following a major flood.

Brunton was a large, imposing man, but to me appeared to be somewhat disheveled. He appeared at Philmont wearing a dark green Explorer uniform adorned only with the silver patch of the Chief Scout Executive, a civilian belt with the tongue end sticking out and curled up, along with a pair of work boots covered with paint spatters.

I was part of a delegation at the Villa Philmonte, a large and elegant Spanish-style home built and occupied originally by Waite Phillips who donated the ranch to the BSA, when Brunton was staying there. A couple of us decided to visit the master bedroom suite, where he was housed. The doors were open and the place was a mess. Clothes draped all over, socks on the floor. I suppose his wife dressed him and took care of those matters at home.

On the other hand, I was impressed by the fact that when he and Tom Watson, President of the BSA (and IBM) visited the ranch, they actually ate a dinner from the trail food menu eaten by the Scouts who were hiking Philmont's Baldy Mountain (14,000 feet). The dinner was specially prepared by a couple of experienced Philmont staffers who were hand selected for the job. I don't know what they really thought of it, but trail food of the 1960s would have made the notorious MREs (meals, ready to eat) of today's military look like a dinner at a five-star restaurant.

Brunton was born in 1902 and became an Eagle Scout, the first Chief to grow up in Scouting and be an Eagle. Joe joined professional Scouting at an early age. He served in a number of councils as a field man and Scout Executive.

While he was the Scout Executive of Chester County Council, he was instrumental in founding Octoraro Lodge of the Order of the Arrow, an organization which will be described in the next chapter, and became a charter member of the 22d lodge founded. Joe became a Vigil Honor member of the OA and was elected National Chief in 1936. Today, the National Chief is always a youth member. From 1944 to 1952, Joe served as Scout Executive of Greater New York Councils, the largest in the country.

In 1952, Brunton joined the national staff and in 1957 became National Director of Church Relations. Since churches are the largest sponsors of Scouting, the job would have been extremely important and probably required some knowledge of various religious groups.

An old clipping shows that Joe was a founding member, along with his parents, of Elfinwild Presbyterian Church in Elfinwild Station, Pennsylvania, in August of 1912. He would have been ten years old. A more recent bulletin of Elfinwild Presbyterian tells us that a Boy Scout Troop was founded at the church in 1923, and that 21 year old Joseph Brunton, Jr., was selected to be its' first Scoutmaster.

Brunton's tenure as Scout Executive was marked by tremendous growth in membership. It was during this time that the Exploring program was changed so that Explorer Posts could specialize in whatever interested them, including careers.

Brunton was awarded many honors during his lifetime, including the Silver Buffalo, 1978, and the Bronze Wolf of the World Scout Organization in 1965.[50]

Chapter Seven

The Order of the Arrow

E. Urner Goodman and Carroll A. Edson

Sometimes in Scouting, as elsewhere, the stars align at a certain point and something unusual and different arises. The Scout Movement itself happened like that and so did the phenomenon known as the Order of the Arrow, in 1915.

Goodman and Edson are placed together because of their joint claim to fame: the foundation of a national honor camping society, The Order of the Arrow (OA). The Order of the Arrow was for many years a major part of Boy Scouting and undoubtedly a factor in keeping older boys as active members of the organization.

The two men who founded the Order, particularly Goodman, were major figures in early Scouting. Goodman hailed from Philadelphia, where he became a Scoutmaster in 1911. He started the first Boy Scout troop in the city.

He became a professional in 1915 and served until his retirement in 1951. He took a leave of absence in 1917 to serve as a Lieutenant in the U.S. Army. After retirement, he was named National Field Scout Commissioner, a volunteer position in which he served actively until his death.

E. Urner Goodman had a distinguished career, serving as Scout Executive in both Philadelphia and

Chicago. Chicago was at the time one of the premier Scouting cities in the country. In 1931, he became National Program Director at headquarters in New York and later New Jersey. Part of his job was to oversee the writing of the Boy Scout handbook, *Handbook for Boys,* and the *Scout Fieldbook,* both written by his friend, Bill Hillcourt.[51]

Another part of Goodman's job was public relations and he really had an opportunity to shine when the BSA decided to hold a national jamboree for the first time in 1937. A jamboree had been scheduled for the summer of 1935, but a polio epidemic caused a last-minute cancellation. Goodman was responsible for the event itself, which was centered on the Mall in Washington and attended by 25,000 boys and leaders from all over the country.

It was a monumental success for the BSA and such celebrities as President Franklin D. Roosevelt and broadcaster Lowell Thomas, showman and author of *With Lawrence in Arabia,* visited the event in the nation's capitol.[52] Jamborees had been held in other countries and been attended by American Scouts, but this was the first time for the world to see that the BSA had come of age.

Goodman was selected in 1941 to oversee the funeral of Daniel Carter Beard, who had died just a few days short of his 91st birthday. Beard remained very popular among boys and leaders in Scouting, and had been a member of the Religious Society of Friends, or Quakers, so his funeral required some sensitivity by Goodman. Boy Scouts and members of the general public lined the funeral route and Scouts handled traffic direction and crowd control.

Like other Scout Executives of his time, Goodman served as camp director in the summers. In 1915, he was director of Treasure Island Scout Camp, in the Delaware River, not far from Philadelphia. His assistant director was Carroll A. Edson. Edson was from Massachusetts and grew up in New York. Like Goodman, he got involved in Scouting as a young man. He was a Scoutmaster and had planned on a career with the YMCA, but was sidetracked when James E. West arranged for him to interview the Scout Executive of Philadelphia, Walter S. Cowing.[53]

Edson went to work as a Field Commissioner in Philadelphia in 1915.[54] Edson and Goodman were the same age, 24. The two men were aware of honor camping organizations, such as Firecrafter, which will be explained in another chapter, in other Scout camps. In fact, almost all Scout camps of the time seemed to have some kind of traditional camp badges and ceremonies based on Native American or local lore, to designate long-term campers.

Goodman and Carroll thought it would be appropriate for Treasure Island to have something of its own. Since the area was rich in the history of the Leni Lenape tribe (and since its language had been put in dictionary form by Moravian missionaries), they chose legends and language from them as the basis for the lore of their organization. Any good fraternal organization for boys and young men must have lore, legends, impressive rituals and secrets known only to its' members. The Order of the Arrow came to have all of these and more.[55]

Unlike most societies of this kind, candidates for membership in the Order of the Arrow are selected each year by members of their own Scout unit, both those in the society and those who have not been selected.

The Order of the Arrow, or "OA," was intended to recognize those who are honor campers and exemplify the best qualities of Scouting, regardless of rank (although candidates must be at least First Class Scouts) or position. The lodges created in each council would elect and be governed by youth member officers, under the guidance of adult advisors.

OA gained popularity across the nation and in 1948 became the official National Honor Camping Society for all Scout councils across the nation, except for the very few that use Mic-O-Say or Firecrafter as their only honor society (or, they could choose none at all).[56] The lodge of the Philadelphia council is the Unami Lodge and is OA Lodge number 1. Each year an event called the National Order of the Arrow Conference, or NOAC, is held in a central location and attended by thousands of young men.

An award and a scholarship have been named after Dr. Goodman (his doctorate was honorary, but people used the title as a measure of respect). His speeches were a major feature of every national OA national conference until his death in 1979.

E. Urner Goodman was one of the last of the remaining early figures in Scouting and, during the 1950s and 1960s he was sought out by Scouts and Scouters, including many of the young men that he helped throughout his lifetime. Right up to the end of his life, Urner Goodman continued to interact with the young Order of the Arrow members at conferences and other gatherings.

A separate book could be written just about the impact of the Order of the Arrow on boys in Scouting. Seton had founded his organization on the history, traditions and lore of the American Indian. The term "Native American" would not come along until much later. Those programs had great success and had Boy Scouting not appeared, might be good programs for boys today. Good, but not major. It seems very unlikely that any boys program that did not include all the possibilities for activities that the BSA offers would have had the major impact on youth of the country that Scouting has.

In OA, Native American lore continued to thrive and was often enormously attractive to, especially, teenage boys. Much money and time were spent by members on costumes and learning of intricate dance routines. Conclaves are still held locally throughout the nation and boys from all over a geographic area come together to dance, sing, drum and trade colorful OA uniform patches for a weekend.

It was always fascinating to hear a bunch of teenagers sitting around a drum and a fire, sometimes literally all night long, singing old songs of the Native Americans. It was once not at all uncommon for boys to remain a part of Scouting into their college years, just to be a part of OA. Many of the male members of Venturing, including Sea Scouting, joined up to keep their OA membership and participate in lodge and area activities.[57]

Native American lore continued to be an integral part of Scouting through the years, but has declined recently, partly due to sensitivities of and regarding people descended from those original Americans whose arrival predated history–although they, too, are emigrants on this continent. However, this age of mass media and especially electronic media, with all the characters a boy can create and manipulate on a computer, means that things like Native American lore are not as exotic to them as to earlier generations. The Order of the Arrow, like other aspects of Boy Scouting, has suffered in recent years from an identity crisis. Interest in drumming and singing has decreased as the focus of young people continues to change.

The Order of the Arrow has also suffered from the fact that it has been largely disassociated with summer camp. From the early days at Treasure Island Scout Camp to the time when the author became a member in the 1960s, OA ceremonies were all held at camp during regular camping season.

In most lodges, boys were selected, or "tapped out," at a ceremony for the whole camp and, placed under strict silence and with an escort, led back to their campsite to get clothing and a sleeping bag for their night alone in the woods.

Next day, campers could see the candidates working on projects around camp, still silent, wearing arrows made of twigs around their necks on which they were on their honor to carve notches if they spoke during the Ordeal, as it was called. Later that night, in a "secret" ceremony, they would be installed as members and given the white sash with a big red arrow that marked them as Arrowmen. When they returned to their troops, they were proud, excited and ready to talk about their experience. All but the "secret" part.

At some point, camp directors realized that this process was interfering which both the teaching and the study of merit badges in camp. Many Scoutmasters and parents like to see their Scouts earn a lot of merit badges during summer camp. The earning of merit badges is a primary requirement to reaching the rank of Eagle Scout. Some, though certainly not all, can be earned only in a camping environment and where an adequately staffed waterfront is available. There are also many merit badges offered at most camps that have nothing to do with camping. A boy really doesn't need to go to summer camp to learn about computers or citizenship in the world.

As time went by, more camp directors started to question the importance of interrupting merit badge studies to do OA activities. The merit badges won and today, OA members or candidates may be recognized during summer camp, but that's all. As a consequence, boys do not see this mysterious, glamorous organization until they are selected to be members.

OA functions are held at other times and only candidates and members attend. It takes away from the aura otherwise created by OA. It also speaks to a question about summer camp in general: Are the boys there to earn merit badges or to have fun and gain experience doing things they wouldn't ordinarily have the chance to do? For boys, fun wins out every time.

Also worth mentioning, although not directly involving professional Scouters, are the Koshare Indian Dancers of La Junta, Colorado.

Since 1933, members of Scout Troop 232 and a related Venturing unit (formerly an Explorer post), have been putting on highly skilled exhibitions of Indian dancing at their headquarters, the Koshare Kiva, and around the country. Although they do the same things as other Scout units, their main theme is Native American lore and the structure of the organization reflects it in all they do.[58]

Chapter Eight

Legends of Professional Scouting

William "Green Bar Bill" Hillcourt

William Hillcourt was born Vilhelm Hans Bjerregaard Jensen in 1900 in Denmark. Scouting came to that country around 1908, and Bill joined as soon as he was old enough. He spent a lot of time doing Scouting activities and earned the Knight Scout badge, the highest award for boys in Danish Scouting.[59]

Sometime in the 1920s, Vilhelm moved to America. He had arranged to have mail sent to him in care of Headquarters, Boy Scouts of America, which was then located at 2 Park Avenue, New York City.

After coming in contact with most of the upper echelon of the organization, he accepted a job with the BSA, one that included working with Norman Rockwell. Rockwell was then art editor of *Boys' Life* magazine, painting magazine covers. It was up to Bill to make sure that Rockwell's paintings got the Boy Scout insignia right and correctly placed.

Later, Bill Americanized his name, moved out to a little house near the lake at Schiff Scout Reservation, married Grace, who was one of the secretaries in the national office and started his own Scout troop. The Hillcourts never had children of their own. Based on his experiences as a Scoutmaster, he wrote several books. One was the *Handbook for Patrol Leaders*.[60]

Patrol leaders were the most important feature of Boy Scouting, both here and abroad, because they were boys elected by a small group or gang of boys to lead them. The patrol is the basic unit of a Boy Scout troop. A young boy of 12 or 13 can effectively lead a small gang and an older boy can manage a larger group made up of these patrols, even without direct adult supervision.

In 1938, James E. West (West's name appeared on virtually every book or pamphlet written during his tenure) wrote in the introduction to a pamphlet, *The Patrol Method, Patrol Helps for Scoutmasters*, "The Patrol Method is something unique. It is a distinguishing feature in the game of Scouting. It is in itself accountable for much of the success of Scouting, because while it does not in any way detract from the relationship of the Scoutmaster to the boy individually, it does make possible the values that come from relationships with a small group. The members of the Patrol, under the leadership of a boy as a Patrol Leader, are all keenly alert for the things which are for the common good of the Patrol; all keenly alert, if wisely led, and ever watchful, as to the welfare and well being of each member of the Patrol."[61]

No other country had yet developed a book for these boy leaders. When Baden-Powell first visited Schiff he wanted to see Hillcourt because he realized the handbook he was writing would influence the movement in America for years to come. They became friends and stayed in touch until the Founder's death in 1940.

Bill, as mentioned earlier, also wrote the *Scout Fieldbook*, which was filled with knowledge he gained as Scoutmaster and pictures of his own troop in their activities. It was possibly because of his standing with B-P and his ability to write these books that made him feel able to stand up to James E. West. Or maybe it was his Danish upbringing.

For many years, Bill wrote a column in the BSA magazine *Boys' Life*, under the byline "Green Bar Bill." Two green bars on the uniform sleeve were the insignia of a patrol leader in those days and the column was written to give the boys helpful hints as to how to have interesting activities for their patrols. He was widely known to boys and adults because of that column and was known to all as Green Bar Bill.

It was Bill Hillcourt who made the observation to me and others that Scouting was a game for boys (not original, B-P always said it was a game), but unlike other games for boys it was designed for them. When boys play Little League, he said, or Pop Warner football, the field is cut down from the size adults play on. The rules are altered to make the game less difficult for shorter legs and less powerful arms. Scouting on the other hand, he said, was designed from the start to be just for boys and just the right size.[62] What he didn't say, but fully intended, was that we tinker with it at our peril.

In the 1960s, he wrote the biography of his friend and mentor, Lord Baden-Powell of Gilwell, who had died in 1940, in collaboration with Baden-Powell's widow, Olave. Because of that relationship, Olave Baden-Powell donated most of her late husband's Scouting memorabilia to the BSA, rather than the British Scouting organization. Lady Baden-Powell was also upset with the British Scouts Association because of program changes they made which were very similar to many of those the BSA has made in the years since.[63] She died in 1975. Bill's wife Grace had died in 1973, but Bill kept on going. He died in 1992, aged 91, while on a world tour to promote a reprinting of his book in many languages and to visit the former Iron Curtain countries where Scouting was now again taking hold after decades of suppression by the Communist governments.

In his later years, he was the only remaining figure from the early days of Scouting. Bill attended all American Jamborees and was invited to travel around the country to attend local events. He would go anywhere for a real Scouting event as long as the trip was paid for and preferred staying with families to hotels. He was regarded by many as crotchety, because he did not suffer fools gladly and, even in old age, did not appreciate having his time wasted. In reality, he was a very pleasant man to spend time with and did not mind sharing Scouting stories that he must have told hundreds of times.

He was also a very gracious and appreciative houseguest. Bill and I ended up staying with the same people at one event. He had a guest bedroom to himself and had gone to bed while a few of us had stayed up to go over some last minute details. A great pounding noise was heard in the bedroom. The door soon opened and Bill appeared, in pajamas. At the same instant, a cat shot out of the room. One of the home's resident cats had been under the bed and didn't want to spend the night there, so it had pounded on the door to be let out. Although he obviously had been asleep, Bill didn't seem to be annoyed.

When he attended events, he would stop and chat with groups of boys, and could still entertain them with little tricks that never got old. One of his favorites was to show boys that he could tell the exact time with a toothpick or small stick that he would stand up in the center of his palm like a sundial. He would observe the shadow, give the exact time of day and the amazed boys never realized that he was wearing a watch, flipped around so that the dial was facing up just like his palm.

It was my privilege to know and spend time with Bill Hillcourt between 1987 and his death. He was just as sharp then as he undoubtedly was in the 1920s and it was a great pleasure to have known him.

During his lifetime, Hillcourt was awarded the Distinguished Eagle Award and the Silver Buffalo of the BSA and the Bronze Wolf award of the World Scout Movement.

James Austin Wilder and Sea Scouting

You couldn't make up a more romantic figure than James Austin Wilder to be a major figure in the start of Boy Scouting in the United States.

James "Kimo" Wilder (Kimo means "Jim" in the Hawaiian language) was born in Hawaii in 1868. He was the son of a prominent businessman, Samuel Gardner Wilder, who had been Prime Minister of the Kingdom of Hawaii under King David Kalakaua, and created a steamship company.

Wilder was a fascinating character, who became a moderately successful portrait artist, and traveled the world at a time when it was slow and dangerous to do so. He lived in exotic places in the South Pacific, Asia and Europe. In his early years, he was a friend and schoolmate of Prince Kuhio (at St. Matthews Cadet Corps, a military school in San Mateo, California) and Franklin Delano Roosevelt.[64] He also once played poker with King David Kalakaua. Wilder lost a large sum of money that he didn't have, but his father bailed him out. An account of some of his undoubtedly exaggerated adventures is found in an enchanting book, *Wilders of Waikiki,* by his daughter, Kinau Wilder.[65]

Wilder could charm his way into and out of almost any situation. He and his wife Sara were renowned as hosts for some of the best parties in Honolulu. Since he could play several musical instruments, including the ukulele, acted in a number of plays and actually wrote a screen play for a Scouting movie in which he starred, it would seem he was more or less a one-man party. The movie can still be found at the Library of Congress.

Kimo was the author of several books, one of which, *Jack-knife Cookery*, was about the art of cooking without pots and pans in the outdoors. He was also known as "Pine Tree Jim," for a book he wrote in 1918, *Pine Tree Patrol*, about the patrol method of Scouting.[66]

When Scouting arrived on the world scene, he was one of the first to pick up the program in the then Territory of Hawaii. He founded the first Scout troop in Hawaii, known as "The Queen's Own." This was not a fanciful designation. The deposed former Monarch of Hawaii, Queen Liliuokalani, was its patron and gave it the motto "Onipaa," or "Stand Firm." Liliuokalani presented the troop with a silk banner with this motto as its flag. The flag is still in the care of the Aloha Council in Honolulu.

A couple of years later, he founded the first Sea Scout Ship in Hawaii, one of the first in the BSA, and Wilder's yacht served as the group headquarters. Shortly after, he answered a call from James E. West to serve as the BSA's first and only Chief Sea Scout. He was a paid member of the executive staff of the national office of the BSA, and thus appears in this history. He wrote the first *Sea Scout Manual*, along with another Sea Scout Skipper and a fellow member of the national staff.

In September, 1922, at the National Conference of Boy Scout Executives, Wilder made a wonderful observation. He said, "There are two places where we never want anybody but our best friends and Scouting has adopted them both, camping and boating . . . Both things, both activities, both adventures call for organized unselfishness . . . [O]n a ship, every man must do his duty."[67]

Kimo Wilder went to England to find out all about Scouting from the men who started it. He later attended the third international Scout jamboree, the Coming of Age Jamboree, at Arrowe Park near London, in 1929.

Upon his return, he suffered a stroke and was an invalid from 1930 on, but he continued to follow the development of Scouting. In 1930, he was presented the Silver Buffalo, the highest award in American Scouting, at the same time as President Hoover and Franklin Delano Roosevelt, then Governor of New York. He could not attend the presentation, but special arrangement was made to get the award to Honolulu so it could be presented to him at the same time as the presentation was made in New York.[68]

After Wilder's death, he continued to be an honored figure, both in Hawaii and in Scouting generally. In 1944, a World War II "liberty ship" was named for him to commemorate his contribution to Sea Scouting. Unfortunately, in later years, Kimo has been largely forgotten. Today, no memorials exist for him, other than at his grave site at Oahu Cemetery, which contains a Sea Scout anchor device with the legend: "James Austin Wilder, Chief Sea Scout, 1917-1934." There is also a stunted pine tree growing there, in an unfriendly climate. Fittingly, his grave is a few steps from the also pretty much unknown grave of author and philosopher Joseph Campbell. I don't think the men knew each other in life, but I'm sure they would have enjoyed each other's company.[69]

Although he has largely been ignored by Scouting historians, Wilder left behind a group of men dedicated to the promotion of Sea Scouting as a part of the national program. One of these men was Commander Thomas J. Keane, USN, who served Sea Scouting as its national director, with time out for World War Two, into the 1950s. Keane died in 1984. It was Commander Keane who became associated with the formation of Sea Scouting in the minds of later generations.

Harold Roe Bartle

Professional Scouter and Mayor of Kansas City

Many will recognize the name of H. Roe Bartle, but not necessarily in connection with Boy Scouting. He is often referred to in his biographies as "larger than life" and having heard him speak in 1962, I would agree with that assessment. He was a huge man with a booming voice and a riveting speaker.

Bartle was educated to be a lawyer, like James E. West, but before long he turned to professional Scouting as his career. He joined the profession in 1923 and served until 1955, leaving only because he was elected mayor of Kansas City.

Bartle had been quite successful in his business and legal pursuits and donated his salary back to the Boy Scout Council during his 30 years of service. He often said there were three Bartles, "the Bartle who makes money, the Bartle who gives it away and the Bartle who works for free."[70]

In Boy Scouting, he was noted for two organizations he was instrumental in founding: Mic-O-Say, an honor camping society based on Native American lore, and which has already been mentioned, and a chapter of Alpha Phi Omega, a national service fraternity for college students who were or had been Boy Scouts, at Parkville College, Parkville, MO.[71] He had a great interest in Native Americans, having been inducted into the Northern Arapaho Tribe as a blood brother during his tenure as Scout Executive in Wyoming. His tribal name was Lone Bear. His nickname was "The Chief." No one seems certain which of his activities brought him the name, but he was National Chief (his title was President) of Alpha Phi Omega for a number of years. Bartle was the mayor of Kansas City who arranged to get the NFL franchise to that city in 1963, and it was for him that the Kansas City Chiefs were named.

The Chief was an amazing figure, a friend to Harry S Truman and other notables. He showed up at major fires as mayor wearing a fireman's hat and coat (another possible reason for his nickname). H. Roe Bartle was a member the board or a trustee of a vast number of organizations. When he accepted an appointment from Harry Truman as Regional Director of the Economic Stabilization Agency, he had to resign from 57 boards of directors to avoid a conflict of interest. During his life, he was the recipient of awards and honors from many of these and from a number of foreign countries. In Kansas City, the convention center is named for him, as is the Heart of America Council Scout Reservation.

His only campaign promise in the mayoral race was to take his honor, integrity, ability and nothing more to city hall. When he made public appearances in Kansas City, he was accompanied by motorcycle police with lights flashing and sirens blaring. He could and did command large fees for public speaking, but for worthy organizations, particularly Scouting organizations, he would speak for free, asking only that he receive a first class airline ticket. Because of his size (at 6'4", he at one point weighed 350 pounds), he only flew first class. A coach seat would not accommodate him, even in those days when seating was more generous than today.

In his later years, he was plagued with health problems, including phlebitis and injuries to his back and legs caused by a 1944 plane crash. Bartle died May 9, 1974, of complications of diabetes and heart disease.

His funeral was attended by the Chief Scout Executive, the Director of the F.B.I. and other notables. Most memorable, however, was the fact the funeral procession route was lined by thousands of young Cubs, Boy Scouts and adult leaders as well as many of the citizens of Kansas City.[72]

Gunnar H. Berg

Educator and Public Speaker

It was shortly after his retirement that I heard Gunnar Berg speak at a council banquet. I was in college at the time and thought he and H. Roe Bartle were the best speakers I had ever heard. I wondered why none of my professors could speak like they did. He was very funny, and used that humor to lead up to a point about working with boys. Most of his public speaking came during his retirement years. Dr. Berg was quite effective, much in demand and it was estimated that he spoke to almost half a million people and traveled well over half a million miles to do so.

Berg was a showman, as well as a public speaker and was director of campfire program for the American contingent at the Third World Jamboree in England in 1929, and director of theaters at the First U.S. Jamboree in 1937.

Dr. Gunnar H. Berg was a Norwegian by birth, but came to the United States with his parents when he was a boy. Born in 1897, Berg earned degrees from three universities, including a Doctorate in Education from Columbia. There is no record of him being a Scout as a boy, but he became a Scoutmaster and held other volunteer jobs in his local council, before becoming Director of Volunteer Training for the BSA in 1927.

Berg was well prepared to be a trainer of Scout leaders. He had worked as a high school principal and taught college science as he was earning his degrees. He also had taught a course in Scout leadership at State Teachers College in Bellingham, Washington.

Like many other professional and volunteer Scouters, Dr. Berg was an outdoorsman. He enjoyed fishing, hiking, canoeing and mountaineering. He probably would have fit in at Philmont Scout Ranch, but his destiny lay with the National Office and Schiff Scout Reservation. He held positions in both volunteer and professional training programs, including serving as Director of the National Training School. Berg was Director of the Professional Training Service at the time of his retirement in 1962.

Dr. Berg retired to Rockaway, New Jersey after his retirement, although he spent some of his time in Florida. He continued to speak for a number of years, and for a few years was resident director of the Humanics Department at Oglethorp University in Atlanta, Georgia. Gunnar Berg passed away in 1987, less than two months after his 90th birthday.[73]

*1910 Formal portrait of Ernest Thompson Seton. Seton is wearing a
British Scout hat badge in his lapel.*

Daniel Carter "Uncle Dan" Beard. Probably taken before 1920, in Scout uniform with the insignia of a National Scout Commissioner.

A group of National Executive Board members and Boy Scouts at the White House in 1915. James E. West is third from right, T.W. Brahenny (not a member of the Board) fourth from right and Colin Livingstone, President of the BSA, in a dark suit next to Brahenny.

Scouts at the Tomb of the Unknown Soldier, Arlington National Cemetary in the late 1920s. The present round-the-clock ceremonial military Tomb Guard did not begin until 1937. The familiar marble cap was added in 1931.

G.H. "Obie" Oberteuffer and Mildred Oberteuffer, ca. 1926.

James Austin "Kimo" Wilder, first and only Chief Sea Scout at a Plymouth, MA, Sea Scout encampment in 1921.

Joseph Taylor, Scout Executive in South Bend, Indiana, 1920s. The first professional Scouter to die in active service, Taylor was drowned attempting to rescue a group of boys whose boat was overturned in a storm.

Lord Baden-Powell, Founder of Scouting and Chief Scout of the World, plants a tree during his visit to Schiff Scout Reservation in the 1930s.

Members of the National Coordinating Committee, 1932. Clockwise from top left: Dr. George J. Fisher, M.D., Deputy Chief Scout Executive, wearing the Silver Buffalo Award; Dr. James E. West, Chief Scout Executive, also wearing the Silver Buffalo; Unidentified; E. Urner Goodman, National Program Director and Founder of the Order of the Arrow; Arthur Schuck, National Operations Director and future Chief Scout Executive; Harold Pote, National Personnel Director; Unidentified.

1937 Jamboree, Washington, DC. The highlight of Scouting in the BSA at the time. Left to right: Daniel T. McManus, Boy Scouts of Canada; E.S. Martin, BSA Director of Public Information; E. Urner Goodman, who was primarily responsible for the Jamboree; Walter W. Head, BSA President; Dr. James E. West; Arthur Schuck; Harold Pote.

The Manor House at Schiff Scout Reservation. The house was part of the original property. Many other buildings were added over the years.

A member of a National Training School class in the 1940s looking at an original Norman Rockwell painting.

Lord Rowallan, Chief Scout of the British Commonwealth and Empire, speaks to a class at the National Training School in the Memorial Room at Schiff Scout Reservation in 1946. Rowallan, a veteran of both World Wars and future Governor General of Tasmania, was an excellent example of the class of British nobility that built Scouting in that country and its Empire without a large professional corps.

Chief Scout and former Chief Scout Executive James E. West speaks to a group of professional trainees in the Memorial Room at Schiff Scout Reservation with Lord Rowallan in 1946. This would have been one of West's last public appearances.

Dr. Gunnar Berg and Chief Scout Executive Arthur Schuck with the Tait McKenzie statue Ideal Scout at Schiff Scout Reservation in the late 1940s or early 1950s.

Wlliam "Green Bar Bill" Hillcourt, 1900-1992, at the BSA Jamboree in 1989, Fort A.P. Hill, Virginia, his final jamboree.

Joe Davis

Director of Camping at Philmont Scout Ranch

I first met Joe Davis (his father and mother were Syrian, but Americanized the family name) when he was the Director of Camping at Philmont in 1965. A unique and almost overpowering personality, he had a singular handshake. Everyone who ever shook hands with Joe knew to beware, because when he grasped your hand, he pulled you toward him in a way that totally threw you off balance. Supposedly, that habit and the strength came from his rowing days at Cornell. But many Scouters, especially the old-timers, had some idiosyncratic gimmicks just for fun. I always thought it was his signature act.

Joe began his Scouting career as so many professionals do, as a 12 year-old Boy Scout in 1924. He became an Eagle Scout in 1928.

Davis graduated from high school in the middle of the Great Depression and could find no job, so it was suggested to him that he go to college. Joe went to Cornell and talked to the Dean of Admissions for the forestry school. While he was sitting in the man's office he noted, among all the photos and certificates, a picture of two boys in Scout uniform. The dean informed him that the Fall class was not only full, but over booked. Still, he asked why Joe thought he would like to be a forester. Joe answered that enjoyed the outdoors and had many woods skills developed in Scouting and that he was an Eagle Scout. The dean then responded that one of his sons had just received his Eagle award and that he thought he could find a place for Joe in the class after all.

Joe graduated from the Cornell School of Forestry. He then went into a Great Depression jobs program, the Civilian Conservation Corps, working for several years in the Catoctin Mountains in Maryland, doing reforestation, building roads and a water supply, much of which still exists. The area where he worked and the facilities he built are now well known as Camp David, the presidential retreat.

He left in 1943 to become a professional on the staff in Philadelphia. While on the staff of that council, Joe was camp director at Treasure Island Scout Camp, which was the oldest camp used by Scouts in the U.S. (It was not solely a Scout camp when founded). Davis later served in councils at Washington, DC, Roanoke, VA and Chicago.

In Chicago, Joe was Director of Activities, which included overseeing the camping properties. During his tenure there, he served as director of legendary Camp Owassippe, the oldest Scout camp in the U.S. It is still operating at the time of this writing. So, in his lifetime, Joe Davis served as director of the two oldest Scout camps in the country in addition to being one of a short list of men to be Director of Camping at Philmont Scout Ranch.

Davis was selected in the spring of 1965, following the sudden death of "Skipper" Junker, who had been director for some years. He was assisted early on by Jack Rhea, who had been director just prior to Junker, to familiarize himself with the ranch. However, Davis learned most of what he needed to know by talking to the permanent Philmont staffers who had spent many years on the property. From the beginning, he also was willing to listen to experienced summer staff, many of whom had also been at Philmont for years. It was a trait that everyone noted in dealing with Joe: He genuinely listened to even young guys and their ideas. He might not agree, but he gave a fair hearing to suggestions, complaints and explanations (as I discovered once when having to give him the facts about an incident that had occurred under my auspices while working there).

Joe Davis' first year at Philmont, and mine, is today known as the "Year of the Flood."

Just prior to the start of the camping season there was a lot of rain in the area for several continuous days. In mountainous country, rain in one part of an area can run down and collect in streams and reservoirs in other places until they all overflow. The water then goes, sometimes very quickly, to the lowest point it can find. This happened in June, 1965, at Philmont. It rained almost continuously on various parts of the ranch for several days. Annual rainfall at Philmont is normally about 12 inches. During just a couple of days, parts of the ranch got 27 inches!

At the time, and probably today, the summer staff of Philmont arrives and spends about 5 days at Camping Headquarters getting trained, briefed and equipped for their summer in the hills. The last day is known as "Operation Scatter." On that day the staffs of the camps all over the large ranch (over 400 square miles) and their equipment and food are driven or packed in to their campsites. These are usually sites with cabins for the staff and some are quite large with a number of buildings for different activities.

Late afternoon and early evening of that day, the flood started. All the water that had been building up in the hills for days was unleashed on the ranch. Normally dry stream beds and washes turned into raging rivers. The main bridge between Camping Headquarters and the southern part of the ranch was knocked out by boulders and trees carried in the raging waters.

On the road between HQ and the town of Cimarron, a four or five foot wall of water washed at least one car and its occupant off the road. The occupant, a staff member, spent the night in a tree. The small car was never found.

Several camps were flooded out and the staffs escaped on foot to make their way to higher ground. It became a rescue operation overnight to save some of the young men who were in particular danger. Fortunately, no one was lost or even seriously injured, although some spent hours in fear. Over the radio from one camp, sound of boulders in the stream could be heard, finally tearing off the kitchen of the building.

Directing the whole operation was Joe Davis. Always calm and reassuring, driving his four wheeler where it could help, talking on the radio to cut-off camps and then, the next day, trying to get the ranch functional again so that when the young campers arrived for the experience of a lifetime, they would get it. Hiking itineraries that had been planned for months had to be changed. Staff members had to get out and hike all the trails on the ranch to see which ones could still be used. It was a monster operation for a new man on the job to oversee. Somehow, Joe and the staff made it all work. Campers arrived and went on hikes and the other activities of the ranch continued, maybe not quite as usual, but it all worked.

Joe remained Director of Camping at Philmont until 1973. During those years there were many changes in Scouting and at the ranch. Joe proved innovative and, as usual, willing to listen to ideas of others. There were many young men who spent numerous summers at Philmont and from time to time had ideas for changes to the program. Davis' door was always open to them and he listened with a willing ear.

One of the major changes that had to be dealt with was the introduction of girls, not only as members of Venturing crews, but also as rangers. Rangers are a large part of the staff and very important to incoming crews. Each crew arriving at the ranch is assigned a ranger, who helps them get checked in, prepared for the trail and then accompanies them for their first few days on the trail. Many old-time Scouters coming to

Philmont were not happy to see a young lady in uniform as their ranger. Davis, however, made sure they were adequate to the task and soon female rangers were commonplace (and popular) in crews and staff.

Joe had a great influence on many young men who served as staff members at Philmont during his tenure and after. He truly loved Philmont Scout Ranch and attended a staff function as late as August, 2008.

I well recall that after my last summer season at Philmont, I was called to active duty in the Air Force and ended up at MacDill Air Force Base in Tampa, Florida. It was rather a pleasant place to be stationed during the war in Vietnam, but a little lonely in the beginning, and quite different than my college days and Scouting summers.

During my first year there, Joe Davis came to Tampa for some Scouting function. I contacted the council office and left my contact information with them in case Joe was inclined to call. In fact, he did call and we had a very pleasant conversation which boosted my morale considerably. I always thought that was a very thoughtful thing for him to do. I saw him again at Philmont in 1968 and at that time was able to tell him how much it meant to me.

Joe left Philmont to become National Director of High Adventure Programs. For the remainder of his professional career, Joe traveled the nation, promoting all the high adventure opportunities offered by the BSA.

Davis retired from professional Scouting in 1978 and returned to Frederick, MD. Rather than live in quiet retirement, however, Joe became a council volunteer and was very active in Scouting up to the end of his life. He also helped to found the Philmont Staff Association and was a regular attendee at their functions.

I had almost forgotten until I saw a video of his memorial service that one of Joe's favorite expressions, which was heard several times at the service: "Carry on!" It is also the title of a book about his life.[74]

One of the speakers at the memorial gave a personal recollection from the last days of Joe Davis' life. Joe had been taken to a hospice, no longer able to eat or drink. He remained in good spirits, however, and having visitors. While cleaning out Joe's home, a couple of his friends had found an unopened bottle of vintage whiskey. They brought the bottle to the hospice and Joe told them that it had been given to him over 30 years before by another friend, now deceased.

They opened the bottle and asked if Joe wanted some. His answer was a definite, "yes." Of course, he couldn't drink anything, so after some thought, they got one of the swabs on his bedside table, dipped it in the whiskey and put it in Joe's mouth. Joe sucked it dry and asked for another. He did this several times and enjoyed it greatly. Yet another speaker said that Joe was not a "glass half full or glass half empty" person, but that he was always a "his cup runneth over" kind of guy.

Joe Davis was awarded the Silver Beaver, the Distinguished Eagle Award and the Silver Sage Award of the Philmont Staff Association. Joe passed away peacefully in October, 2008, at the age of 96.[75]

J. Harold Williams

Long-Time Leader in Rhode Island

J. Harold Williams served as Scout Executive of the Narragansett Council, BSA, from 1918 until his retirement in 1962 at the mandatory age of 65. He was, as were others noted in these stories, known as "Chief."

Williams began his Scouting career as a member of the Rhode Island Boy Scouts in 1910. The Rhode Island Boy Scouts was one of a number of local Scouting organizations that sprang up because of Baden-Powell's book, *Scouting for Boys*.[76] A corporation was chartered by the State of Rhode Island and still exists as a trustee organization for property and funds. The Rhode Island Boy Scouts merged with the BSA in 1917.

Williams was a Boy Scout from 1910-1914, and began his public speaking career at the age of 15 at a Boy Scout rally in Rhode Island. At the age of 18, he became a Scoutmaster, serving until 1918, when he became the Scout Executive of what was then the Greater Providence Council, BSA, now Narragansett Council. Under Williams' leadership the council became the largest in New England.[77]

The official magazine of the BSA, *Boys Life Magazine*, was established by an 18-year-old Providence entrepreneur, Joseph Lane. Apparently the magazine was received enthusiastically by Scouts everywhere, because the BSA purchased it from Lane in 1912 and has published it ever since.

Donald North was hired to serve as the first Scout Executive in 1915 and left to become Scout Executive in Boston in 1918. An interim Scout Executive served briefly until 21-year-old J. Harold Williams was employed to be Scout Executive and camp chief. The National Council would only accept him provisionally and he was considered an acting Scout Executive. Meanwhile, Williams commenced to work closely with the non-professional men who had established the council and built the Scout camp, Camp Yawgoog. The camp was enlarged and improved several times over the years. In the early 1930s, all four councils in Rhode Island, Newport, Pawtucket-Central Falls and

Woonsocket merged with Greater Providence Council to become Narragansett Council, covering the entire state.

A feature of this era in many councils was what is called Scout shows or Scout circuses, where boys from all units can compete and show off Scouting skills to the public. These were held in a public auditorium until they grew so large they had to go outdoors. In those days, before television and movie mega-plexes, these kinds of spectacles attracted lots of people for entertainment value. Today, they attract mostly proud parents and friends of Scouting, but they are still held in many places. The oldest continuously operating Scout show is the Makahiki, still held every year in Honolulu.

In May of 1930 when a forest fire burned much of the forest land at Camp Yawgoog, it became an opportunity for Scouts to work at reforestation, planting seedlings that are today a beautiful forest. A hurricane in 1938 struck Rhode Island. The Scouts were ready. They mobilized by troops and did rescue work, messenger service, traffic direction, security of property, salvage, water distribution and much more. Williams estimated that 2000 boys in uniform worked during the emergency.[78]

In 1941, the surprise attack on Pearl Harbor, Hawaii, and declaration of war by Germany put the entire U.S. on a war footing. Many Scout leaders and former Scouts went off to World War II. During these years, Scouts did some amazing work. All over the country, they collected wastepaper, aluminum, handed out pamphlets, put up recruiting and bond drive posters, rounded up books to send to GIs overseas, harvested crops, acted as airplane spotters and many other wartime tasks.

Boys who were probably longing to serve at the front were able to serve the nation at home. There was a program called "War Service Ace" that enabled

Scouts to earn a ribbon for doing a certain amount of war work.[79]

After the war, Scouts in Rhode Island and others across the nation sent what they could to their fellow Scouts in war torn Europe and the Pacific.

In 1947, the first post-war World Jamboree was held at Moisson, France. At the next, in Bad Ischl, Austria, in 1951, Chief Williams was responsible for the arena shows. Williams also produced arena shows at each of the U.S. National Jamborees from 1937 through the Jubilee Jamboree in 1960 at Colorado Springs, Colorado.

James E. West did not appear to have many close, personal friends. He had many followers and correspondents, but his biographers have named few who considered themselves close friends. J. Harold Williams was one who did.

In 1920, West met Williams at a Scout gathering. For some reason, West took a liking to the young man and, upon learning it was his tenth year in Scouting, removed his own ten-year veteran pin and placed it on Williams' lapel. Williams was one of the very few who actually called West "Uncle Jimmy." West had often used this nickname and encouraged youngsters to think of him as "Uncle Jimmy," but most Executives and volunteers called him "Dr. West."

J. Harold Williams was recommended by Dr. Fretwell to succeed him as Chief Scout Executive in 1948. Williams was not chosen. He certainly would have been qualified, but his close relationship with West probably cost him that job. The Chief could have undoubtedly moved up in Scouting anyway, to Regional Executive or to the national staff, but he chose to remain in Providence as "The Chief." Upon his retirement he was given the title of Scout Executive Emeritus (there is no such position on any chart) and remained so until his death in 1976.

It would be difficult to catalog the changes in the world and in Boy Scouting that took place during the lifetime and professional career of J. Harold Williams.

Chapter Nine

The Regional and Council Scout Executives

James P. Fitch

The Donation of Philmont Scout Ranch

Another early Scouter in the U.S was James P. Fitch. Born in 1887, he was a school teacher and somehow discovered Boy Scouting. He began to organize Scout troops in 1910 and 1911, in both cases serving as Scoutmaster. Later, he was engaged in Chautauqua work, an adult educational movement popular in the late 19th and early 20th Centuries, and apparently had some arrangement with the BSA to organize Scout troops along the way. In 1916, Fitch became a District Scout Executive in Chicago, and later in Columbus, Ohio. During his time with the Chicago Council, he served as camp director of Camp Owasippe. In 1918, he became a National Field Commissioner, with responsibility for several states and in 1920 became Regional Scout Executive for Region Nine, which included Oklahoma, Texas and New Mexico.

In his job as Regional Executive, "Jim" met and recruited high-level businessmen to contribute money and influence to the BSA. One of these men was Waite Phillips, an oilman. The result was the donation of his New Mexico ranch, The Philmont, to the BSA, which is described elsewhere. When Jim left Region Nine in 1946, Waite Phillips insisted that he become manager of the Phillips properties, including the ranch and the Philtower Office Building in Tulsa. Fitch stayed in Tulsa until 1951, when he became Deputy Chief Scout Executive in New Jersey. He retired from professional Scouting in 1952 and passed away in 1964.[80]

Minor S. Huffman
Author and Philmont Scout Ranch Manager

Very few of the old time Scouters are as well documented historically as Minor S. Huffman, one of the really major figures in early Scouting in the Southwest United States.[81] Minor Huffman's name comes up in several places in this book and frequently in other histories. He appears to have been a man not only of great abilities, but one who was willing to mentor younger men he encountered. This is a quality that was missing in the later generations of professionals.

Huffman was born in 1900 in Roswell, New Mexico and died there 90 years later. His career began as a Boy Scout in New Mexico in 1913 and lasted until his retirement from Scouting in 1965. He was a member of a troop formed by a "Professor Young" at the Christian Church in Roswell. This troop didn't last long, breaking up when the professor went to California to study law.

Huffman soon became a member of Troop 2 at the Southern Methodist Church. This troop was to be continuously in existence for over 50 years. In 1922, Minor accepted employment with the Chamber of Commerce to provide leadership for Scouting in the Roswell area. He left to work at the Citizen's National Bank, but was also serving as Scout Commissioner, an unpaid position, and managing a clubhouse that the Scouts in Roswell had acquired.

During this time Huffman got interested in Carlsbad Caverns, which then was privately owned and not a tourist destination owned by the National Park Service. It had been mined for guano, which is droppings from the bats who have hung upside down in the caverns for eons, and one of his acquaintances was employed by the mining company as caretaker for the property.

Bat guano, by the way, has been mined for use as ingredients for both fertilizer and gunpowder, and has been quite valuable in the past. Places like Carlsbad had vast quantities of it, which has the additional quality of not being smelly. Great stuff, guano.

Minor arranged to have a group of Scouts guided through the cave and sleep there overnight. The group descended a mine shaft into the caverns by way of a large bucket.

Huffman's friend, Jim White, is credited with being the discoverer of Carlsbad Caverns. It was he who laid out trails and marked out routes that tourists today follow under guidance of the National Park Service.

In 1924, it was decided to create a council for all Eastern New Mexico. A budget of $6000 was raised and Minor Huffman was hired to be the Scout Executive effective January 1, 1925, at an annual salary of $2,700. He later said that, "had [he] known [he] would be asked to write a history of the council fifty-eight years later he would have kept better records of these events."[82]

In 1926, the council was using Camp We-Hin-Ah-Pay in Ruidoso, New Mexico.[83] Almost 100 Scouts witnessed a man fall from a 40 foot cliff where he and another man had been searching for cliff swallow nests. The bottom of the cliff was a mass of nothing but solid rock.

Scoutmasters rushed with a stretcher and the camp doctor was soon on his way, but it was a torturous journey back to the foot of the mountain and into camp. Miraculously, the man was found to have no broken bones and was kept in the camp first aid lodge for observation.

It soon became apparent that the whole thing was a stunt which had been staged to impress on boys the dangers of climbing on the cliffs. It probably had that effect, although one wonders whether it was necessary to subject all those boys to a traumatic event in order to accomplish the job. On the other hand, a lot of boys would consider something like that to be the highlight of their week at camp.

The author has seen many stunts in Scout camps over the years, including a memorable scare concerning a "wild bear" that kept Scouts awake half the night in fear and has never been a big fan of these things regardless of the intent. Boys tend to believe what adults tell them when they are younger, but become somewhat skeptical as they grow older, largely because their innocence has been played upon by adults too many times over the years.

Huffman relates this event without saying whether he had any role in it, but he seems somewhat embarrassed in telling it. Of course, he was a very young man at the time.

Developing the camp in Potato Canyon at Ruidoso was something Huffman really enjoyed. Camp We-Hin-Ah-Pay was 126 acres and Huffman arranged to purchase an adjacent spring that pumped out 32 gallons of freezing cold water per minute. There were some buildings on the property and more were built over the years. The camp expanded and added property and buildings.

Also constructed was a rather unique swimming pool. Some of the staff dug out a rectangular hole, lined it with roofing paper, mopped it with tar and filled it with water from the spring. The only problem with the pool was that the water was so cold that almost nobody would swim in it and a "Polar Bear" award was given for those who did. Eventually the camp acquired the use of a nearby lake that had swimming and boating facilities in order to teach boating, canoeing, swimming and lifesaving.[84]

In 1932, Minor Huffman left Eastern New Mexico to become Scout Executive of the El Paso Area Council, El Paso, Texas. In 1936 he became a Deputy Regional Executive of Region Nine, based in Dallas.

In 1943, Huffman was invited to become the first property manager of Philmont Scout Ranch in Cimarron, New Mexico. The ranch was then over 130,000 acres, which is considered a medium sized property in those parts. It had recently been donated to the BSA by Tulsa oilman Waite Phillips.

The property ranged in altitude from 7,000 to 12,000 feet above sea level, had a couple of sizeable mountains on it, and was an active cattle and horse ranch. Phillips had constructed fishing and hunting cottages at various spots around the ranch.

Phillips was a philanthropist who had contributed greatly to the people of his hometown, Tulsa. In 1934 he contacted the Boy Scouts of America about donating a sizeable piece of his property to Scouting.

The BSA didn't jump in, recognizing the financial and logistical difficulties of such a property, not to mention the unknown factors. One major question at the time was whether any significant numbers of Scouts would make a journey to a relatively remote part of the Southwest. In 1938, however, they decided to accept the gift of 35,857 acres to be known as Philturn Rocky Mountain Scout Camp.

By 1941, Phillips felt that more of the ranch could be valuable to Scouting and offered an additional 90,000 acres, including a large home, the Villa

Philmonte, the ranching operations and buildings around the ranch.

To his credit, Phillips realized the financial burdens this could place on the BSA and tendered the Philtower office building in Tulsa to provide income. At this point, management of the properties became a major undertaking. It was a cattle ranch, horse ranch, training center and expedition base, coupled with a 23 story Tulsa office building.

Huffman inherited a job no professional could have trained for and found himself with something unlike any Boy Scout camp in the world. Scouters from Britain had been amazed at Schiff Scout Reservation's 400 acres in New Jersey! He remained until 1946 and oversaw many changes in the operation. Of course, others in the camping operation at Philmont had to figure out what kind of program to run for boys and how to run it. Given the size of the ranch and the widely varied topography, that must be a story in itself.

By the time Huffman left to become Scout Executive in Sam Houston Area Council, Houston Texas, Philmont had become a top camping program throughout the BSA. Currently boys come from all over the country to hike the trails, ride the horses, try to get burros to haul equipment and participate in archery, high-powered rifle shooting, archeology and improvement projects.

Many thousands of leaders have attended training conferences with their families in the shadows of the Villa Philmonte. The ranch has been added to in the last 50 years as adjoining land became available and now comprises over 400 square miles of land, on which there is a 14,000 foot mountain.

Minor remained as Scout Executive in Houston until he retired in 1965. He continued to be active in community affairs, including Scouting and the Roswell Chamber of Commerce. He also wrote at least two books, *The Saga of Potato Canyon* and *History of Region Nine, Boy Scouts of America 1920-1967.*[85]

In the epilogue of The Saga of Potato Canyon, Huffman wrote, "This program will succeed as long as lives are moulded [sic] by the concept of the Scout Law, The Scout Oath and the Good Turn."[86]

O.A. Kitterman

A Long and Distinguished Career

Oscar Avery Kitterman was Regional Executive of Region Eight. He was born in Vichy Springs, Missouri in 1895. Like many other Scouters of the era, he was originally involved with the YMCA and became an Assistant Scoutmaster in the years just prior to World War I.

He was drafted in 1918 and assigned to a Medical Corps unit scheduled to depart for France. He was stricken by the Spanish Influenza bug, which killed millions at the end of the war, and didn't deploy to France. The Armistice was signed and "Kit" was assigned to Stateside duties until early 1919.

Kitterman became a real estate salesman in Salina, Kansas, and became State Commander of the American Legion, which was a major force in attempting to rid the state of the Industrial Workers of the World (IWW, or Wobblies), a radical, anti-capitalist labor movement. At one point, Kit's name was found on a list of people to be killed by operatives of the union. He would have been next had the killer not been caught.

When the Great Depression hit, Kitterman lost a great deal in previously valuable properties and left the real estate business.

He was recruited into professional Scouting, went to a training school and worked as a professional in

Ardmore, Oklahoma. Kit then moved to Dallas, where he became Scout Executive. He stayed until 1930 and the Circle Ten Council saw a lot of growth, both geographically and numerically, under his leadership.

That year, Kitterman moved to Boston, Massachusetts to be Scout Executive. The council was deeply in debt as a result of the Depression and Kitterman was able to turn it around financially and located the Council headquarters in a nice spot on Beacon Street.

Kit was selected to lead the Region One contingent to the World Jamboree in Holland in 1937. The Jamboree was one of note and had a sad aspect. The world was clearly on the verge of war. Germany under Nazism had no more Boy Scouts, so none attended from there. It was also the last jamboree attended by Lord Baden-Powell, who would soon move to Kenya, where he died in 1940. Many of the boys and leaders at that Jamboree would be lost in the coming conflict.

Kit became the Regional Executive of Region Eight, located in Kansas City, in 1945. He traveled constantly around the six state area served by the Region.

In 1960, Kitterman retired and moved with his wife Ruth, first to Harlingen, Texas and then to Naples, Florida. Ruth died in 1976, but Kit lived on until 1992, when he would have been 97 years of age. He died in Shell Point, which is just outside Naples and his ashes were scattered over the bay.[87]

Gilbert H. Gendall

Scout Executive

Gilbert Gendall was born in 1883. His father was a Methodist minister. Gilbert, after high school, prep school and college, became a secretary to the head of a large coal company and later was executive secretary to one of the daughters of New York financier Jay Gould. He did "boys' work" for the YMCA in New York, prior to becoming a professional Scouter.

Apparently, his initial assignment was to be the first Scout Executive of what is now the Mid-Iowa Council, headquartered in Des Moines. That was in 1916 and he remained there until 1921. He did an excellent job of getting the council on a solid footing economically and program-wise.

When he left to become Scout Executive in Omaha, an award in the form of a cup was established in his name to be awarded to the most outstanding boy member of the council each year. Presumably, the award no longer exists, as no current record could be found of it. It would also be a very difficult job today to select one outstanding Scout from among the numbers that make up Scouting in the various programs of any council.

During this time, the council expanded its geographic boundaries and leased the land on which the first permanent camp, Camp Mitigwa, would be established.

In 1940, after almost twenty years as a professional, Gendall left and during World War II, he worked as an executive for the USO in Rochester. After the war, he went on to be an executive with Big Brothers. He continued his membership in Scouting as a volunteer until he passed away in 1963 at the age of eighty.[88]

Richard Newcomb

Trainer of Trainers

One of the only "old-timers" I got to interview by phone before his death was Richard Newcomb, a boy who joined Scouting and never really left. He joined

Scouting at age 12, became an Eagle Scout and went on to be a volunteer in Louisville, Kentucky. Although he was trained as a civil engineer, he was never able to get a job in middle of the Great Depression. He took a five cent per hour job in the paint company where his father worked. He worked 60 hours a week. Since he was volunteering with the local council, the Scout Executive asked if he'd ever considered becoming a professional. Not having a lot else to do, Dick filled out the paper work and was invited to join. He attended National Training School at Schiff in 1936 as a member of Class Number 51.

His first professional assignment was as a District Executive in Ohio, serving an area around Lorain in what is now the Heart of Ohio Council, BSA. He said that, having had no experience, he just followed the example of the Scout Executive he knew in Louisville. A couple of maxims he got from his experiences were: "Always keep [a volunteer] between you and the problem." This was good advice. By involving a volunteer to deal with another volunteer you avoid having to make policy or involve "council" directly in the problem. Indeed, many such problems go away by following this motto.

Another of his maxims was: "Check out the abilities of people you meet." and "Find the person that's needed to recruit the man you need for the job." In other words, don't grab the first person that's available to take on a particular job, but find one who is equipped and in a position to deal with it. Next, don't try to recruit the man yourself, but find someone that the man will find it hard to say "no" to. Great advice for anybody dealing with volunteers. It may be that these skills were not taught at Schiff in the 1930s. By the time I got there, they were being stressed. This doesn't mean that we always got the point right away. I recall many occasions when I or others settled for a man that wasn't up to the job, usually to our great regret.

It was Newcomb's job as a junior District Executive to count registration certificates. Councils received the certificates from the national office and were required to record each one issued. A fee was paid for each certificate issued. Periodically, a Regional Deputy would come in to count the certificates on hand. If the council had issued more than they reported they had to pay a fee to the national office. Today, of course, registrations are handled by computer directly between councils and the national office.

Dick said that when he was a Scout Executive, he made sure that new professionals were introduced around their district and got to know the volunteers they worked with. He also asked the Council President to be sure they were invited to attend Council Executive Board meetings with the volunteers from their district. That way, the volunteer and the professional worked hand in hand. It was also his policy to advise the new man to never take credit for anything himself. If the professional did it, it meant a volunteer didn't, which isn't the idea. If a volunteer did it, that's the person who should get the credit. Another maxim: "Always wear your distinctions on the uniform of your volunteers."

As with other professionals, when the war came, Dick went to volunteer. With a Reserve commission, he only had a physical exam standing between him and war service. However, since birth he had had a problem with one eye. Somehow, he managed to memorize the eye chart and got on active duty with flying colors. When the time came for his division to mobilize for "Operation Torch," the invasion of North Africa, they were required to take a more extensive physical. This time, he couldn't get the chart and the doctor caught on to his problem. He was sidelined for

the invasion and spent the rest of the war at Camp
Campbell (now Fort Campbell), Kentucky. During the
five and a half years he served, he found time once
again to serve as a volunteer Scouter.

When he was released from active duty, he went
back to professional Scouting, taking a Senior District
Executive job in Toledo, Ohio.

Soon after, he was invited to join the staff of
Region Seven as the junior Deputy. He was part of a
team serving Ohio, Michigan, Indiana and Kentucky.
He soon became a kind of troubleshooter and got sent
to councils that were having problems.

On one of his first trips, he was sent to a council
in Illinois that was stagnant. The council was having
no growth. He was told to relieve the Scout Executive,
but he instead met with man who eventually asked
what he was there for. Newcomb informed him that he
was there to relieve him or get him to get the council
going again. The Scout Executive quickly assured him
that he would get the council going and he did.

One of the opportunities he had during those
years was to work directly with a volunteer Regional
leader who was chairman of Shell Oil in Chicago. Dick
said he learned a great deal from working with a man
of this caliber. The chairman always sent his own
people to get any problem solved directly, rather than
waiting for it to go away or trying to deal with local
people to get it solved.

From time to time over the years, Dick
encountered problems with the Community
Chest/United Fund/United Way (UW), as it has been
over time. On one occasion, the representative came
into Dick's office and said the BSA salaries were out of
line with the local UW guidelines. Dick explained that
salaries were set by the executive board of the council
under guidelines from national council. The man
would not let up and finally, when the next UW check
was supposed to arrive, it failed to appear. A phone

call revealed that they were holding it until the "salary issue" was resolved. One of the things about Scouting is that, if it is working properly in a community, some of the key people from almost any organization will be part of it. In this case, a phone call to a volunteer who was a major figure in the UW resulted in the check being sent and no more was heard about the salary issue.

As is discussed elsewhere, the UW has, in recent years, treated the BSA councils they support rather badly. Rightly or wrongly, UW takes the position that the BSA is discriminating because of its interpretation of the Scout Oath and Law which excludes some from membership. For that reason, they have cut back or cut off funding in many councils. The cost of those reductions has been, in many cases, to force the councils to sell property, usually Scout camps, to make up the budget deficit. This has, incidentally, also cost the UW contributions from people in the community who support Scouting. It is a sad situation and one that will not be resolved soon.

Dick recalls making a visit with another Regional Deputy to meet with a District Executive in Nevada. The man was found at home doing laundry. This didn't go over well with the Regional men who felt it didn't show a great deal of respect. Dick never told me what happened to the man's career. On another occasion, he stayed in the home of a Scout Executive and volunteered to baby sit so the man and his wife could go to the movies, a real treat for them.

From Region Seven, Dick moved south to Region Five. One of his favorite things was running National Camping Schools, required for senior camp staff members in all Scout camps, and Wood Badge courses. Wood Badge has long been regarded as the ultimate Scouting training for adult leaders. The aim of the program is to create leaders who will train not only boys, but other leaders in the methods of Scouting. It was created at Gilwell Park in England under the tutelage of B-P and eventually migrated to the U.S. Dick Newcomb was part of the second Wood Badge course held in the U.S., which was technically a British course and his Wood Badge certificate is signed by John Thurman, Camp Chief of Gilwell in England. Dick served on many Wood Badge staffs during his career.

Dick left the Regional staff because it took him away from home too much. He said that on one occasion, he was re-tiling the floor of his kitchen when he got a call that an emergency had arisen somewhere in the Region and he should drop everything and go. So he left his wife and family with a half-tiled kitchen and took off to solve the emergency.

Eventually, he became a member of the National Field Operations staff at National Headquarters in New Brunswick, NJ. He ended his career as Director of National Supply Service, which is the branch of BSA responsible for acquiring and marketing of uniforms, insignia and other "official" Scouting gear.

When he retired, Dick and his wife moved to Roswell, New Mexico. For 35 years, Dick was active as a volunteer in the Conquistador Council. There, he served as Council Commissioner and directed a number of Wood Badge courses. He was awarded the Silver Beaver in 1981. He moved to The Villages in Florida in 2009 and passed away in 2010. His wife had predeceased him.[89]

Stanley A. Harris

Pioneer of Interracial Scouting

Stanley A. Harris was truly a pioneer in Scouting in this country. He was born in 1882 in Johnson County, Tennessee. He graduated from Tennessee Wesleyan

College in 1903 (other sources say he attended Aaron Seminary in North Carolina and graduated from American University in Harriman, Tennessee) and taught school for a while before going to work for the YMCA.

Living in Frankfort, Kentucky, "Stan" was an outdoorsman and frequently led hikes for young boys from the "Y." In 1908, he read about Baden-Powell's Boy Scout program and applied for and received a charter from B-P to establish a Boy Scout Troop.

Two years later, when the BSA was established, Stan received a commission as Scoutmaster from that program. Two years after that, he was made a special National Field Commissioner, which was a volunteer position, and organized Boy Scout troops all over Tennessee. During this time, Stan was of service in establishing what is assumed to be the first all-African-American Boy Scout troop in the U.S. He also was involved in the founding of the first troop of Native Americans in the U.S.

In 1917, Stan joined the professional service of the BSA as a National Field Commissioner, with responsibility for 14 southern states. Six men across the country in what became 12 Regions held similar positions at the time. In 1920, with the establishment of Regions, Harris was assigned to Regions Five and Six, with particular responsibility for Region Five. He was the first Regional Executive for the Deep South states.

In 1926, Stan apparently suggested to West that the BSA needed an arm to extend Scouting into the African-American community. At any rate, he became first director of the BSA Interracial Service, an initiative to help bring more African-American youth into Scouting. As a result of his efforts working with these youth, Stanley Harris became the first white person to receive an honorary degree from Tuskegee Institute.[90]

Stan retired from professional Scouting in 1947, as Assistant Director of Operations for the BSA. He moved to Boone, North Carolina, where he worked as executive secretary for the chamber of commerce for 15 years. He remained active in local Scouting until he was confined to a nursing home, where he died in 1976.

The North Carolina Office of History and Archives erected a marker on U.S. Highway 321/441 in Boone, commemorating him as a Boy Scout leader and founder of the Interracial Service of the BSA.[91]

Spurgeon P. Gaskin

Scouting Visionary

Spurgeon P. Gaskin was a well-known figure in Scouting in the Southeast United States. He retired from professional Scouting after serving as the first Regional Director of the Southeast Region of the BSA. To meet him, you would think he was the most easy-going typical Southern gentleman you would ever find. He *was* a gentleman and had an easy manner, but he was a highly motivated leader who could see beyond the horizon.

"Spurge" was born in 1911 in Ocilla, Georgia, but at some early point in his life, moved to Jackson, Mississippi. There, Spurge became a Boy Scout at age twelve. He reached the rank of Eagle Scout when he was 13. We also know that he worked as a staff member at Camp Kickapoo, near Jackson, because an uncle of mine, who also became an Eagle Scout, told me he worked with Spurgeon on staff in the 1920s. Spurgeon was one of about a dozen Scouts nominated from around the country to go on an expedition with Commander Richard Byrd to the South Pole in 1926. Only one young man, Paul Siple, was selected to go.

Spurge later graduated from Millsaps College in Jackson, and went to work for the Mississippi State Highway Department as a Civil Engineer. He served as a Scoutmaster, Troop Committeeman and member of the Andrew Jackson Council's Executive Board. He was part of Troop 8, which is still active in Jackson.

In 1936, Gaskin went to work for what is now the Andrew Jackson Council as a Field Executive for the area around Hinds County, where he organized 23 Scout Troops in about a year's time. He, of course, also had to raise funds for the work. In 1937, he was made Assistant Scout Executive in Oklahoma City, where his primary job was to work with the newly started Cub Scout program for younger boys (ages 9-11 at the time). He accomplished a great deal in organizing and training people to work as volunteers in the program. He was working with two other men, one of whom later became the National Director of Cub Scouting, and these men literally wrote the books on Cub Scouting. In 1939, Spurge was offered the job of Council Scout Executive in Buffalo Trail Council, West Texas. There were relatively few boys in Boy Scouting there, no Cub Scouts and, because of the Depression, no money. In the next few years under Spurgeon P. Gaskin, membership increased dramatically, Cub Scouting was introduced, five new staff members hired and the council was financially able to maintain a reserve fund.

World War II came along and, in 1944, Spurgeon was commissioned a Lieutenant, Junior Grade in the Navy. Not much of his war record has been found, but he was a combat officer aboard an amphibious vessel. At the end of the war, he was offered a promotion to Commander if he would stay in the Navy but, instead, Spurge went back to the BSA.

In 1946, he became Director of Field Service, supervising 19 men in a fast-growing council. He particularly excelled in staff organization and financing. It is Spurge who was credited for creating a system of work scheduling for professionals that soon was in use almost everywhere. It is not certain what method he used, but the concept involved a day-book calendar scheduler, like an early version of Day-Timer® or Day Runner®, where professionals could plug in important future dates at meetings and then "backdate" steps that were necessary to accomplish the job. The field men could then put their daily schedules, appointments and meetings, into the calendar. Although those scheduling meetings were the bane of our existence, because it took days to complete, we had a backdating conference every year. They are extremely important for efficient functioning in that kind of business. Today, much of this is computerized.

In 1952, Spurge became Scout Executive in Raleigh, North Carolina, where membership was at 6,000. Under his leadership, the figures five years later were 18,800. He built a new camp, a new, modern service center and the council was recognized for growth, quality and membership by Region Six.

In 1961, Spurgeon Gaskin became the Regional Executive of Region Six, which then took in North and South Carolina, Georgia, Florida and the Canal Zone. During his thirteen-year tenure, Region Six won the Lorillard Spencer award, which was an award for excellence among the twelve regions, 8 times and placed second or third in the other years. In 1971, Spurge raised five million dollars to be distributed among councils in the region where there were large numbers of disadvantaged youth, primarily rural, placing a professional in those councils whose only purpose was to work to organize and train in disadvantaged areas.

In 1972, the regional structure of the BSA was changed and the number of regions reduced. The newly created Southeast Region, headquartered in Atlanta, included eleven Southern states, Washington DC and the Canal Zone. Spurgeon was selected to head this new Region.

During his tenure, Spurge accomplished much, but possibly his most notable single achievement was the establishment of a High Adventure Gateway in the Florida Keys. Established in Islamorada, the Florida Sea Base operates year-round and offers thousands of young people, age fourteen to twenty-one, a chance to sail and dive some of the most beautiful waters around the mainland U.S. Spurge was smart enough to find the late Sam Wampler, the young South Florida Council Director of Camping, to move down to the Keys and get things started. No one could have done a better job of establishing this new experience for youth than Sam, who unfortunately passed away in 2002. Attendance is so competitive, that the base staff has to determine attendance each spring, for the following calendar year, by a lottery.

During his tenure, the region led the whole country in membership growth, which was an important effort during that era of Scouting. Boypower '76 again. In 1975, Spurgeon retired from professional Scouting and continued to live in Atlanta until his death in 2005. Spurge was Regional Executive during the entire time I was a professional Scouter and I can say that he was highly regarded and genuinely liked by all who worked with him. Morale in the region was consistently higher, as was work product, under his leadership than in the other regions of the country.[92] After his retirement, Spurgeon was awarded the Distinguished Eagle Award, the Silver Beaver, the Silver Antelope and the Baptist Scouting programs' Good Shepherd Award.[93]

George J. Fisher
Volleyball and Boy Scouting

You've probably *never* wondered how the sport of volleyball became so ubiquitous in this country. The reason has a lot to do with Dr. George J. Fisher, who was Deputy Chief Scout Executive from 1919 to 1943 and a National Scout Commissioner until his death in 1960.

Dr. Fisher was a medical doctor, who was president of the Physical Director's Society of the World YMCA in the early Twentieth Century. During America's involvement in World War I, Dr. Fisher was Secretary of YMCA War Work. Around 1914, Dr. Fisher worked to get volleyball included in the educational and recreational program of the U.S. military. As a result, everybody in the Army learned to play volleyball. Dr. Fisher was the editor of a book of rules for the sport for the use of the armed forces. American soldiers played volleyball during training and recreational time while in the U.S. and Europe during the War.

Fisher had been a volunteer Scouter since 1910 and had chaired the Committee on Badges, Awards and Scout Requirements. He wrote a section on "Health and Endurance" for the 1911 Boy Scout Handbook. Just about the time Fisher joined the National Staff, the BSA began a 5 year program to organize the country into local councils, which would be part of larger regions. A system of quotas for fees from councils had to be established in order to pay the salaries for the regional people. Many councils either wouldn't or couldn't contribute what National thought to be fair, so National Executive Board member Mortimer Schiff, contributed $100,000, and later offered to pay the $6000 annual salary of one Field Executive in each of the twelve regions, if the region would match it. By the end of the Twenties, there were over 630 local councils headed by professionals.

Professional training became important. Scout executives were told that they "should read a daily newspaper, a weekly news digest, book reviews and at least one book a month, including great literature such as the Harvard Classics. [They] should do in-depth reading or take courses in a related topic such as psychology or business and should attend conferences and summer schools."[94]

During his time as Deputy Chief Scout Executive, Fisher, along with E. Urner Goodman and of course Bill Hillcourt, served as counterpoint to James E. West's sometimes autocratic style of leadership.

Dr. Fisher received numerous honors and recognition in the U.S. Volleyball Association and the Silver Buffalo of the Boy Scouts of America (1926).[95]

"Coach" Anderson

A Scouter's Scouter

Nashville, Tennessee, was one of the pioneer cities in aggressively organizing the Scout movement in the U.S. In 1920, a board of citizens had incorporated what is now the Middle Tennessee Council, BSA, and, after a diligent search, selected William J. "Coach" Anderson.

Anderson was sent to a five-week training experience at Springfield, Massachusetts and later attended a conference of Scout Executives at Bear Mountain, New York.

An office was opened in Nashville in September, 1920, and the council started looking for qualified men to be Scoutmasters, even advertising in newspapers for volunteers.

Anderson retained his job at Vanderbilt University, where he worked as track coach until noon each day. He spent afternoons at the Scout office, handling paperwork and talking to prospects on the phone. He spent many of his evenings prospecting and training.

The council acquired and set up a summer camp in 1921, and thereafter Coach Anderson spent every summer heading up the camp for the 27 years he led the council. Boys would ride streetcars out to a point where Anderson, driving the camp's one truck, would meet them and carry them to camp. Anderson would meet with his secretary, who had come out on the streetcar with the boys (and who, incidentally, was probably running the council by herself in Anderson's absence), and deal with paperwork while the Scouts waited. There was no phone at camp, but in 1938, a volunteer set up an amateur or "ham" radio station at camp and another at the office in Nashville so they could keep in touch.

To those who are familiar with today's Scout camps, a 1930s camp would look familiar, but some things were different. For one thing, today's Scouts largely go to camp with their own troop under their Scoutmaster from home. In those days most boys signed up for a week or weeks and lived under the leadership of the camp staff.

The staff of those days was, like today, composed mainly of high school and college age boys. Sometimes the camp director was the only real adult in camp. Today's Scouters (and parents) would be shocked at the difference in safety precautions by comparison to today. Many boys went barefoot in those days and nobody thought anything of it. Of course, if there were serious accidents the boys could be taken to a hospital, but most things short of broken bones were handled by whatever first aid skills were available at camp. They did use the "buddy system," adequate trained lifeguards and other special precautions on the waterfront, even in those days.

When the Great Depression hit in 1929, funds went down by about half in Nashville. The Council was unable to pay Anderson very much of his already meager salary. So, he kept on the job and survived on his earnings as a track coach.

In the 1930s, funds may have been lousy, but Scouts were plentiful. Kids adapt to pretty much anything and Scouting was cheap for them in those days. Anderson ran the council with the assistance of one secretary all through the Thirties.

He recruited Scouts to come into the office to fold and stuff envelopes, lick stamps and run errands. Apparently, Coach also did all the training of leaders, a six-week course meeting one night a week, by himself, for a long time. All this while coaching track at the university. He had a lot of ceremonial duties to perform, most of which were on nights and weekends. It's hard to imagine what kind of home life he might have had.

In 1938, Anderson finally got an Assistant Scout Executive, James Gribble. Gribble was an Eagle Scout from a local troop and had been an Assistant Scoutmaster.

A system of volunteer Scout Commissioners had been established in 1934. It was their job to take over some of the training and ceremonial duties Anderson had been doing.

In his newly created "spare time," Coach would go around to outlying areas with other Scouters to help them organize new Scout councils as well.

Anderson had to deal with expansion of Scouting to kids in two new groups. Scouting had been and continues to be populated largely by middle class white kids. Anderson and some others wanted to see it expand to African-American kids and what would later be called "underprivileged" kids.

Segregation was not only the social norm in the South in those days, it was the law. So, black kids had their own troops and, usually, their own Scout camps. Contrary to what you might expect, most of the organization, training and funding for these "Negro" children came from white folks. They successfully brought many boys in both categories into Scouting during those days.

Anderson and some others came up with the idea of getting police and firemen to run a program for the poorer kids. During World War II, they made sure the African-American and underprivileged kids' troops kept on going, along with running scrap metal drives, war bond efforts and other support for the U.S. war economy.

After WWII, Coach Anderson got a letter from an Italian Scoutmaster, explaining that his Scouts were without uniform shirts, which he felt was vital to their organization. Anderson started a drive in Nashville to collect used Scouting equipment of all kinds, including uniforms. Scouts would clean the uniforms and equipment and drop them off at a downtown store, where they were packed and shipped off to Italy.

Coach Anderson retired from Scouting in 1947, making a farewell speech in which he lamented that he should have done more for Scouting. He coached track for another year before retirement from Vanderbilt.

Anderson died in 1963. There is an athletic field at Vanderbilt University named in his honor, but, despite the fact that more than 100,000 boys passed through Scouting under the tutelage of Coach Anderson, apparently there is no memorial to his Scouting achievements.

Bill Hillcourt often said of Baden-Powell the words that appear under the dome of St. Paul's in London as a monument to its builder, "If you would see this man's monument, look about you." The same could apply to Anderson and men like him. He was typical of a hardy breed of people with a work ethic that today is hard to find at any price.[96]

Joe Taylor

An Early Loss to the Profession

Joseph "Joe" Taylor was a University of Louisiana graduate who was hired to be the first Scout Executive at Akron, Ohio, in 1916, at a time when there were 200 registered Scouts in the community.

Taylor was known as an outdoorsman and he put a lot of emphasis on camping among the troops.[97] We don't know much more about Joe Taylor, except that he was the first professional Scouter to perish while an active member of the movement.

He was the Scout Executive in South Bend, Indiana in the early 1920s, described by his peers as a "vigorous, enthusiastic, virile, progressive Scout Executive."[98]

Sadly, Joe Taylor was drowned in an attempt to save the lives of four boys. Taylor, the four boys including Taylor's ten-year-old son, and two Scoutmasters were boating on a large lake, when the weather turned rough and the boat capsized, drowning all occupants.[99]

Taylor's funeral was the largest-attended funeral in South Bend history at the time and his widow was the first recipient of a benefit from the Scout Executive's Alliance.[100] The people of South Bend showed their appreciation by over-subscribing the council budget for the next year.

Francis Oliver "Chief" Belzer
Founder of Firecrafter

An old-timer with an interesting story was Francis Oliver Belzer, of Irvington, Indiana, who was known as "Chief". In 1911, Belzer, who was teaching at a local college and C.C. Osborne, met with a group of Irvington boys to form Troop 9, sponsored by the Irvington Methodist Church.[101]

He became president of an association of Scoutmasters and helped to found a Boy Scout camp. In 1914, the Central Indiana Boy Scout Council was formed and selected Belzer to be its first Scout Executive. He held the job from 1915 until 1940. Like the other old-timers, he spent a lot of his time recruiting and training Scoutmasters, saying, "If we had a hundred more Scoutmasters, we would have a hundred more Scout troops tomorrow."[102]

Belzer went with eight American Scouts to the 4th World Jamboree near Budapest, Hungary, in 1933. He was a friend of Uncle Dan Beard and learned about Beard's pioneer program. Apparently, it was this program that gave him the idea to create a camping society, which later became known as Firecrafter, at Camp Chank-Tun-Un-Gi, which, in the language of the Native American Miami tribe means "a loud, happy place." Firecrafter was a "secret" society, with rituals and solemn ceremonies and a system of camp ranks that could be earned by its members while at Scout camp. This program would be recognized by most of today's Scouters as a parallel of the Order of the Arrow. While Firecrafter was never recognized throughout the BSA like OA, it still exists.[103]

Belzer retired in 1940 and died in 1948 at the age of 79. Camp Chank-Tun-Un-Gi was later renamed Camp Belzer in his honor.

The National Capitol Area Council
Scouting in the Nation's Capitol

Though not enough information is available about individual professional Scouters in the Washington, DC, area to do a biography of each, the council itself figures so prominently in the history of the BSA that it would be impossible to leave out some of its history. From February 8 to October of 1910, the BSA was headquartered in that city and much of its organizational activities took place there. James E. West started his career as a Washington lawyer. Originally named District of Columbia Council, the National Capitol Area Council loomed large in early BSA history.

Scouts in Washington participated in some of these activities, such as the First Annual National Council Meeting, held at the White House in 1911. In March of that year, almost 300 Scouts held a demonstration of Scouting skills which was attended by two thousand people.

The Washington, DC Council was organized in June and Ernest S. Martin was selected to be "Scout Commissioner," later "Executive Secretary" and still later, Scout Executive of the council.

Martin, who had started the first Scout troop in Colombia, Ohio, and held Scout Masters Certificate number 197, issued in September, 1910, was a high school principal and Superintendent of Playgrounds for Washington. He also held positions with the American Red Cross and was coordinating agent for the U.S. government to the BSA. In short, he was ideally placed to take the council to prominence very quickly.

In February of 1912, General Baden-Powell visited the United States and included Washington, DC in his itinerary. Martin arranged a White House reception for him and later a dinner in his honor at a private home.

It cost the council about $500 (over $12,000 in today's economy) to host B-P, none of which was repaid by anyone. Nevertheless, it was a huge feather in the cap of Scouting in the District of Columbia.

A council summer camp was held that summer, but it was rather unsuccessful and only one season of camping took place there. In the next two summers, Washington and Baltimore held a joint camping season at a camp on Chesapeake Bay. The Washington council bought the 60 acre site in 1914 and it was named Camp Archibald Butt. Colonel Butt had been a military aide to President Theodore Roosevelt who was a major figure in supporting early Scouting. Butt had died in the sinking of the *RMS Titanic* in 1912.

In 1913, local Scouts were honored for work in snow removal for Woodrow Wilson's Inauguration as president. Following that, the council served at every presidential inauguration through the end of the Twentieth Century.

Ernest Martin worked with those who were pushing a Congressional Charter for the BSA through the houses of Congress and had the honor of calling James E. West at 4:10 a.m. to tell him the charter had been approved after a lengthy delay in various congressional committees.

Martin was soon called to New York to work in the national headquarters of the BSA as secretary of the Editorial Board and assistant secretary of the Court of Honor. In this job, he was responsible for working on the development of badges, awards and Scout requirements for those awards.

H.H. Grogan was hired to replace Martin as Scout Executive and served from 1915 to 1918, a particularly interesting time in Scouting because of the Great War (later World War One, 1914-1918) in which the U.S. was involved from 1917 to 1918. Martin continued to serve as government and BSA relations coordinator and found many ways for Scouts across the country to serve during the war. The fledgling Scout Movement had much difficulty in negotiating public feelings about the war, which separated the "peace-at-any-cost" camp from the "war now" movement. In the end, the country felt there was no choice but to enter the fray and Scouts at home were doing all they could to support the effort.

The council camp didn't operate in the years 1916 through 1918. It reopened in 1919 under the name Camp Theodore Roosevelt. A member of the council staff, Linn C. Drake, served as camp director during summer camps. Drake became council Scout Executive in 1918, but continued to oversee the camps. In 1920, the council was given 46 acres of land which became the Woodrow Wilson Boy Scout Reservation. This camp operated until 1951 and was sold off in parcels.

Another camping society arose at Camp Roosevelt around 1921. It was called The Clan of the Mistic [sic] Oak (CMO) It was much like the Order of the Arrow, except that a council of adults governed the organization. The CMO declined during World War II and in 1952 was officially dissolved and replaced by the OA.

In 1926 the Washington DC Council hosted the Founder once again. B-P, now Sir Robert Baden-Powell, who had been unmarried due to his military career and Boy Scouting until this time, brought along his new wife, Olave, Lady Baden-Powell. Both B-P and President Coolidge gave addresses that were broadcast nationally.

The National Jamboree scheduled to commemorate the 25th Anniversary of the founding of the BSA, was set to take place in Washington DC in 1935. Of course, a heavy burden was placed on the Washington DC Scouts to prepare for and perform duties during the Jamboree. There was great disappointment when the Jamboree was cancelled, literally at the last moment, because of a polio epidemic. The Jamboree was rescheduled for 1937 and all the preparation had to be done again. This time the event came off with splendid results and the Washington council and its Scouts distinguished themselves in front of the nation and the world.

In 1938, a resolution was passed to change the name of the corporation to the National Capital Area Council, BSA, in recognition of the wider areas surrounding the city that were served by the council. At the same time, the national office had adopted a retirement program for Scout professionals, which was incorporated into the council procedures. At the time, employees of the BSA were not included in the newly enacted Social Security Act and thus would have had no retirement at all without this new program.

In 1938, King George VI and Queen Elizabeth of Great Britain visited the U.S., the first time a reigning British monarch had ever done so. Four or five thousand Scouts greeted the King and Queen and performed for them on the White House lawn. Scouts also were involved in traffic control, after special instruction from police, and acted as emergency first responders for heat prostration during the parade from Union Station to the White House. This was an especially propitious visit, coming as it did on the eve of World War II. The King, who was 44 years old, formed a good opinion of the United States and its president, Franklin Delano Roosevelt, who during their stay at the White House often called him "young man." King George was able to serve as an example to his people through some really dark days in coming years and his relationship with Americans became vital as our country assumed a major role in the fighting.

In 1943, Linn Drake, Council Scout Executive, broke his leg and was unable to perform his duties. During this time, Rock M. Kirkham was acting Scout

Executive. In early 1944, the executive board was informed that Mr. Drake's health might preclude him returning to his old job. Later that year, Drake sent a letter to the board advising them that his retirement was due on September 1 and was given leave of absence until that time.

At his retirement, Drake was honored for his years of service and for the tremendous accomplishments and growth of the council on his watch. During the years of his leadership, growth was tremendous, both geographically and in numbers. Linn Drake headed the council through two world wars, a depression and oversaw great changes in the National Capital Area Council. The council was always in the national limelight and never failed to perform.

This council was one of the first to begin to deal meaningfully with the "Colored Scouts," and even had an African-American professional before WWII. Although segregated, black Scouts were able to find troops and leadership as well as summer camping from an early date. There were a large number of African-American Eagle Scouts in council.

Clarence F. Urferr took over as Scout Executive September 1, 1944, but he wasn't there for long. In March of 1946, Urffer was appointed Regional Executive of Region Three, in Dallas. He was replaced by Kenneth Spears as Executive of the National Capital Area Council.

Ken Spears was soon faced with some major challenges. The Arlington District applied directly to the national office to be granted status as a separate council. Apparently, there was no consultation with the National Capital Council prior to the application, and to say there was shock and hard feelings would be an understatement. The application was rejected by the national office. It's easy to imagine the amount of time and effort on the part of the professional staff required to smooth the ruffled feathers during that time.

Spears was also faced with financial problems. The Washington Community Chest, predecessor of the United Way, could not fund the council needs. According to the funding agreement, the council then had to request permission from the Community Chest to raise the difference between Chest funding and council needs. The Community Chest was not happy with the prospect, but under threat of council withdrawal, it was agreed that the Scouts could raise the money needed.

Spears left the council in 1951 to be recalled to active duty in the U.S. Air Force for the Korean War.

I close this chapter by paying homage to a man who served as Scout Executive, National Capital Area Council, BSA in the late 1990s.

Ron Carroll served as Scout Executive in Central Florida Council during the 1980s, where I got to know him. He accomplished quite a lot in the Orlando area and established a great relationship with the Disney management. Ron moved on to DC in 1990, where he served until his early retirement in 2005. He was able to accomplish many things in Washington, including acquisition for the Scouts of some Virginia property belonging to Disney. Disney had envisioned a theme park there, but plans were rejected due to historical concerns about the proximity of battlefields and grave sites from the War Between the States.[104] Ron had terminal brain cancer and died shortly after his retirement, at the age of 59.[105]

Ray Matoy
Transatlantic Council

When I was a teenage Boy Scout, my father was assigned to an Army Division that was transferred to Germany. There was no Scout troop in the little outpost near Nürnberg (Nuremberg) where we were, but some officers soon got one going. I think my dad, who had briefly been a Boy Scout himself, might have had something to do with it, but he never said so.

Later, I had the opportunity to go to a meeting of the Transatlantic Council, BSA, (TAC) at the Army recreation center at Garmisch-Partenkirchen, Germany. We encountered some of the professional Scouters of the council there, including the council Scout Executive, Ray Matoy.

I still have a clipping from the event and the names of the executives taken from the *Stars and Stripes* newspaper.[106] I was somewhat surprised when I began researching this book to find Matoy's book, *Thunderbird Tracks*. Written in 1987, it is a history of the Will Rogers Council, BSA, and of some of the men who mentored Matoy as he went through Scouting and became a professional. It's a great read, and although I've never even been in that part of Oklahoma and am unfamiliar with the names of most of the men who made Scouting happen there, the story is fascinating.

Ray Matoy was a Boy Scout in 1933 when he chanced to meet Deputy Regional Executive Minor Huffman. He later served as camp director of Camp Cee-Vee-Cee in 1939, when he was twenty, and was selected to be director of the council Camp-O-Ral, a weekend camping event, often called a camporee, with competitive games and joint campfires for Scouts, shortly thereafter.

Matoy then became a professional Scouter on the staff of the Cimarron Valley Council in 1940 before going off to World War II as a Second Lieutenant in 1942.

WWII caused many councils to be short-handed and coincided with a prewar growth of membership that needed service. A lot of volunteers went off to war as well, but Scouting continued to thrive throughout and emerged stronger than ever when the men came

home. Of course, many men who had served as
professionals, volunteers or been Boy Scouts did not
come home and many troop flags were adorned with
memorial stars to honor members and former
members who died for their country. That practice
continues in many troops today, with stars added for
lost Scouts who served in Iraq and Afghanistan.

Matoy was one of the lucky ones who returned
and served the council again, becoming Scout
Executive in 1946. In 1947, the Cimarron Valley and
North Oklahoma Councils agreed to merge in order to
better serve the units in that area. An operating
budget of $31,000 ($255,000 in today's dollars),
including $17,000 for five professionals and two office
workers was approved for that year. Mr. Matoy was
interviewed and selected to be the first Scout Executive
of the new council. A committee was formed to select a
name for it and decided to name the council after Will
Rogers, possibly the most nationally famous figure
from Oklahoma.[107]

There is a process that has been repeated time
after time across the country. When Scouting began in
the U.S., everything happened in the neighborhood.
Scouting was no exception. As time went on, and
especially after WWII, people began moving to the
suburbs and commuting to work. In the early days,
rural youth were served by the Lone Scouting program
already described. One farm boy, miles from anyplace,
could be a Lone Scout and get at least some if not all
the benefits of Scouting without a troop around.
Today, of course, there are very few places so isolated
that they can't get to a community in a few minutes by
car. We live in era of "urban corridors" and "metro
areas." It makes sense for councils to be
geographically larger, since they can benefit from the
resources of more professionals and more top level
volunteers. Driving back and forth is a way of life, so
driving someplace for a training event, camporee or

council meeting is not a big deal. So councils have been merging for a long time and larger areas are being served from a central office. The Aloha Council in Hawaii serves boys as far away as Samoa and the Marshall Islands. The Far East Council, headquartered near Tokyo, serves American boys in Japan, Korea and some other outposts in the Pacific Basin. The Transatlantic Council, as will be seen, covers a far-flung group of American Scouts in Europe.

In 1956, Matoy accepted the post of Scout Executive, Transatlantic Council, headquartered in Heidelberg, Germany. At the end of WWII, the U.S. Army never left Germany. First there was an Army of Occupation to pacify and organize a denazified government. After the Federal Republic of Germany (West Germany) was established, the U.S. Army remained as a part of the North Atlantic Treaty Organization (NATO) to deter the Soviet Union from attempting to take over West Germany as it had East Germany, Poland, Czechoslovakia, Hungary and everything east of there. The Army began bringing over family members and setting up schools for dependent children shortly after the war. Scout units began almost immediately and were served directly by the National Council, BSA. By 1950, there were so many dependents and so many Scout units that a council was established in 1953 to serve them. At the time, it was essentially funded by the U.S. Army Europe, which had a good recreation services budget.

It must have been a great job for a professional Scouter to have. Although most professionals have some opportunity to travel abroad for international Scouting events, few have the chance to go and live for several years in Europe. It was also in a way like a sabbatical. No fundraising to do. Volunteer recruiting is not as difficult, since volunteering in community activities is a way of life for military families. Council employees were paid by government as though they were serving members of the military. They had access to military housing, commissaries, post exchanges, schools and medical benefits. Few, if any, councils inside the contiguous 48 states could have had such a deal.

At the time Matoy came to TAC, it served boys in Germany, England, France, Spain, Italy and smaller outposts like embassies as far away as Moscow. I recall during the council meeting going to a seminar in which the professional Scouter conducting it mentioned that he served and lived on a military installation in Spain, which at the time was ruled by Francisco Franco, a Fascist. Scouting was illegal in Spain and although U.S. military Scouts and professionals were not bothered on their military reservations, there were times when the Spanish police would detain them if they were in Scout uniform off base. This gentleman had actually spent a day or two in jail as a result of one such incident.

American Scouting in Europe was not quite the same as it was in the U.S. Most Americans lived in housing areas that were separated from the German community. Of course, there were smaller numbers of boys in the Scouting age groups. Still, looking back, I'm surprised more kids didn't join Scouts, because there wasn't all that much to do. There was no TV for Americans in most of Germany. Armed Forces Network (AFN) ran local stations in only two areas. Otherwise, there was German TV. Not very good and it was in the German language, which most American kids didn't bother to learn. I became a fairly fluent German speaker, but never got used to German TV. AFN ran radio stations everywhere, so you could listen to "stateside" music and news in English. On base, movies changed two or three times a week and were very cheap. Boys over ten had to wear jackets and ties to get in. Every base had a bowling alley and everybody went bowling. My first real job was as a pin setter at the base bowling alley. There were snack bars where you could get a good old American hamburger with fries and Cokes. Some large bases had youth centers where kids could hang out. Others allowed kids into the service clubs. Either place would have cards, ping-pong, pool, music and other staples of American life. Still there wasn't all that much to do. Maybe it was the weather that kept them out.

Weather in Europe is notoriously lousy. It was almost a given that any major Scouting event would bring in storm, rain, snow or ice. The Fiftieth Anniversary Camporee in 1960, celebrated on the same date throughout the BSA, to commemorate 50 years of Scouting in the BSA, was held at Munich for our district. Although it was late July, it was rainy and cold and everybody froze. The German Scouts in attendance thought it was grand because the Army fed us and they wore their lederhosen shorts with sandals every day.

Matoy left the Council sometime after 1960 and went to Four Lakes Council in Wisconsin. He was still there in 1971, but must have retired and returned to Oklahoma. In 1994, he received the Silver Beaver in that Council, so he apparently was retired and working as a volunteer.

Ray, in his nineties, is still alive at the time of this writing. He wrote to me in 2009, having just left a hospital bed. He didn't write much, but he did send copied article about "America's First Boy Scout Troop" in Pawhuska, Oklahoma. It doesn't deal with professionals, but it's a worthwhile story of Scouting history and I will share a bit of it here.

In 1909, an Anglican Priest, Reverend John Forbes Mitchell, was assigned to a church in little Pawhuska. He had served with Robert Baden-Powell, as an aide and chaplain, during the Boer War in South Africa, where B-P so distinguished himself. Mitchell had also worked with B-P in England in the early stages of the formation of Scouting.

Reverend, or Father, Mitchell applied to B-P for a charter and received it in July, 1909, eight months before the BSA was incorporated. He organized the nineteen boys he recruited into a drum and bugle corps and ordered uniforms from England.

Walt Johnson, one of the original members, later said that the uniforms cinched the deal with the boys. They were filled with desire to be Scouts. The troop followed the British program to the letter, including singing "God Save The King" (the British National Anthem) to the amusement or consternation of parents. The troop later received charter number 33 from the BSA.

The Osage County Historical Society has a commemorative statue, an exhibit and a granite marker listing the names of the boys who were original members of the troop. Their British charter and other archives are in the museum. Whether they were actually the first American troop to be chartered is far from clear, but it is a historical footnote of great interest in the history of Scouting.[108]

Will Fuller

An Early African-American Professional

Although I had worked alongside Will, I didn't have much information about him. Thanks to the new movie *Red Tails*, I discovered a bit more of his history. In 1970, he was an older (by my standards), African-American District Executive in South Florida Council in the 1970s. He was a great guy to sit and have coffee with. I knew he was a private pilot and found out after a while that Will was one of the famous Tuskegee Airmen.

Willie Howell Fuller was born in Tarboro, North Carolina in 1919. He received a B.S. degree from Tuskegee Institute and went from being a student to enlisting in the Army shortly after Pearl Harbor. He was selected to be in the first company of Tuskegee Airmen, which was an experiment to see if Negro soldiers, as they were known, could match the flying skills of white pilots. Many Tuskegee Airmen flew fighters in Europe during World War II, in segregated units, and many of those units distinguished themselves.

Will flew with the 99th Fighter Squadron in the European-Mediterranean Theater. He flew 76 missions and received the Air Medal twice. His unit participated in the liberation of the island of Pantellerea. He remained in the Army Air Force until 1947, which was coincidentally the year that President Harry S Truman ordered the desegregation of the U.S. military forces.

Will then returned to civilian life, married and worked with his wife's family in business, before starting his own taxi service company in Georgia. He became active in Boy Scouting and was hired at some point in the 1950s to be Scout Executive for the Negro Division of West Georgia Council, BSA. In 1960, he moved to the South Florida Council, where he remained until his retirement. Will died in 1995 and was buried in Miami.[109]

When he joined professional Scouting, there were few African-American professionals. It's a tribute to the man that he was willing to push the outside of the envelope, not just in the air, but as a member of society.

John Haien
Dayton Professional

Scouting came to Dayton, Ohio, only after a great deal of effort. There were men designated as National Field Scout Commissioners who went to areas having problems organizing. These were men trained to raise money in order to hire Scout Executives and set up offices. Twice, two of these commissioners went to Dayton and twice they failed.

Many early Scout Executives or Council Commissioners were good at program but weak in financing. These usually ran out of money and left, unpaid for their efforts. In 1918, Arthur Roberts went to Dayton, found some key supporters and had a lunch meeting to raise some money. Roberts had to go the extra mile to get them to cough it up, but they did. Only when he, himself, laid a $100 Liberty Bond, representing 25% of his entire net worth (about $1500 today), on the table and turned to leave, did the men at the meeting realize that the stranger had faith in their community and they should, too.

They formed a council, the Dayton Council, BSA, and got together the Scoutmasters and others who were already running Scout units without benefit of council support. Through the National Council, they found John Haien, who was selected to be the first Scout Executive.

Roberts stayed around Dayton until he was due to report for service in the Army, and assisted in raising funds. Haien was no slouch, however. He was a Harvard man and had taught economics, but he understood what his job in Dayton was.

One principle he understood very well was the value of what we today would call "PR." When any troop went camping, Haien made sure it got in the paper. He was obviously a "boy-man" and often went on campouts with troops. He managed to obtain land for a farm to be run by Scouts with profits going to the council and later more land for a Scout camp.

By late spring of 1918, Haien had work going on at the new camp. He discovered an old baseball stadium was being torn down and worked out a deal to get the lumber in return for supplying boy labor. With the lumber they were able to construct a large building on the camp. Those kids must have had some serious calluses by summer, but they had a camp.

Like other councils in the country during World War I, Dayton Scouts were encouraged to do war work, including selling Liberty Bonds and collecting peach pits, which were used to make gas masks for the soldiers.

Membership grew at a rapid pace. Soon, the council staff was increased by one. H.W. Sinclair became the first Council Commissioner. It isn't clear if he was paid, but he worked directly with the troops, freeing up some of Haien's time for other matters.

A council-wide camp was held on a weekend at Triangle Park and Scouts demonstrated Scouting skills to the public for the first time. Messages were sent around by semaphore and Morse signals, fires were built using friction and bridges were built using lashings. To test the bridges, a Ford Model T automobile, which weighed about 1200 pounds, would be driven across it. None failed.

Late in 1918, the Spanish Influenza came to Dayton as it spread across the U.S. and around the world, killing millions. Twenty-one thousand died in the U.S. during one week of the pandemic.[110] Scouts were called into action to help the Red Cross finding blankets and sheets, working in hospitals and carrying messages.

In the winter of 1918-1919, there was a boy named William Perkins who nagged A.W. Payne of the West Side YMCA to organize a Scout troop. Payne had not been able to decide to commit himself. One night young William went to a local theater where a "mystic" from exotic India was answering questions from the public. The boy of course asked the mystic if Mr. Payne would organize a Boy Scout troop, which brought the house down. However, the mystic said, "Yes." The same night Mr. Payne decided to start the troop and made plans for its first meeting which took place in July.[111]

In 1920, John Haien dropped by to see Perle "Whitey" Whitehead, principal of the Fairview School. Whitehead had been the organizing Scoutmaster of the newly formed troop at the school. Whitehead had been active with the YMCA and had served in combat during World War I. He also worked with low income kids at the Irwin-Springfield Street Mission. Haien needed a new professional and thought Whitehead was just the man. Whitehead didn't need much encouragement to come on board.

Also in 1920, John Haien decided to undertake a major adventure. He would take a group of experienced older Scouts into the wilds of Canada. Scouts had to enter a competition to be selected. Tickets were sold to the competition, which was called The Round-Up, and enough money was made that Haien decided the selected Scouts would not have to pay anything to make the trip. He was overly optimistic.

The group left Dayton in early August and boarded a Pullman car on a train bound for Canada.[112] They switched to a Canadian railway and continued to a stop in the middle of the wilderness about seventy miles into Canada. From the railway station, they hiked about five miles in to a site on the shore of Spruce Lake, accompanied by wilderness guides and set up a camp.

For a week the Scouts hiked, canoed, swam, fished and visited an abandoned mining camp. They hiked out and took a ferry to Mackinac Island, Michigan, where they had planned to stay at the Grand Hotel. Anyone who has ever seen the movie, *Somewhere in Time*, starring Christopher Reeve and Jane Seymour, will be familiar with this hotel, which is the centerpiece of the film. Unfortunately, they were extremely short of funds by this time and couldn't pay the hotel, but the manager allowed them to sleep on the spacious lawn provided they didn't put out their sleeping bags until after dark. The paying guests were not to be disturbed by Scouts camping on their lawn!

Next day, they were supposed to take a ferry to Detroit, but again were without funds. At the ferry port, St. Ignace, the Scouts put on a show, doing songs and demonstrating fire-making techniques and managed to raise enough money to buy ferry tickets. They had to do another show aboard the ferry to get money for food and rail fare. They got enough just to get seats, no Pullman berths, and returned to Dayton ahead of schedule. No one was expecting them early, so the trip ended with the boys hiking back to their homes with all their gear. It was a memorable trip and without doubt any of the boys would have done it again the next summer.

These early trips demonstrated that kids would do almost anything to get what Scouting now calls "high adventure." Today, the BSA has Philmont Scout Ranch, the Florida Sea Base and a couple of wilderness canoe bases in Minnesota and Wisconsin that older youth can experience, with costs and transportation set in advance. In today's Scouting, a leader must submit a trip plan in advance, indicating methods of travel and names of leaders. No adult would, of course, be allowed to take a group of boys into the wilderness alone.

The *Dayton Journal* began putting a full page in the Sunday edition, edited by Perle Whitehead. Scout troops would submit items about what they were doing and helped keep Scouting before the public.

There was one Scout who contributed first rate cartoons for the Journal page on a regular basis. His name was Milton "Milt" Caniff. If you are old enough, you'll remember the comic strips "Steve Canyon" and "Terry and the Pirates," both by Caniff. They were features of daily newspapers across the country into the 1960s. It was through his cartoons in the *Journal* that Milt was recognized as having talent and encouraged to develop it. Caniff became an Eagle Scout and was an active figure in Dayton Scouting during the 1920s. Caniff was later given the Distinguished Eagle Award, which is presented to a select few Eagle Scouts who have done outstanding work in their profession and community. Caniff also provided illustrations for the council history book by Warren R. Hauff, *Fun and Service, A History of the Boy Scouts of America in the Miami Valley Council.*

In 1922, economic times were hard, although not as hard as they were to be nine years later. However, in view of the larger territory John Haien had to cover, it was thought prudent to buy him a car. At first the executive board suggested that a far more inexpensive motorcycle would serve, but Haien put his foot down and held out for the car. A used one was bought for $730.00. Just a year earlier, the Board had voted to increase Whitehead's salary from $30 to $40 a week.

In October of 1922, John Haien resigned as Scout Executive and Perle Whitehead was made acting Scout Executive and later Scout Executive. In later years, this practice was prohibited by the National Council to prevent undercutting and competing among the staff. Often a man would leave his council to serve in another so that he could return when the current Scout Executive retired.

Perle "Whitey" Whitehead

The Miami Valley, Ohio, Council

Perle "Whitey" Whitehead continued the council growth begun by Haien. In the summer of 1923, President Warren G. Harding died suddenly while traveling on the West Coast. A special train carried the body to Washington and then back to his hometown of Marion, Ohio. Scouts in Dayton were called upon to provide an honor guard for the coffin while Harding lay in state.

Dayton has long had a close association with aviation. It was here that Wilbur and Orville Wright had their bicycle shop and designed the first working airplane. The brothers were used to boys hanging around the shop and liked to work with them, so Orville was willing to be a merit badge counselor for both Aviation and Cycling Merit Badge. As a result, many boys in Dayton had an opportunity to spend time with this aviation legend while earning their badges. Aviation was quite popular around the country and certainly in Dayton, which had Wright-Patterson Army Air Field (now Wright-Patterson Air Force Base) just a few miles away.

In 1924 the World Air Races were held at Dayton and the council offered to provide Scouts as ushers. About 1500 would be needed, so Whitehead had to recruit Scouts from all over to get enough boys. An encampment had to be set up, food provided and other facilities, but Whitehead managed to get it all done.

The races were a great success and the Scouts were able to add a feather to their caps for a job well done. Later, in 1927, Charles Lindbergh was making a triumphant U.S. tour following his New York to Paris solo flight and Perle Whitehead led a delegation of Scouts to welcome him to Dayton.

One of the other pioneers of Dayton Scouting was Fred Rike, president of Rike-Kumler Department Store. In 1926, he suggested that, as a way of promoting Scouting, uniformed Scouts could take over running the store for an hour and a half on a Saturday morning. Although it was be a busy time in the store, boys took over all positions, including president and were joined by Girl Scouts. Cash results aren't known, but the store did not go under after that day. One result was that the boys and girls learned a lot about retail business on that Saturday.

Another James E. West story unfolded in Dayton, during a meeting of Region Four he attended in 1928. West called Whitehead in his usual peremptory way at six p.m. and ordered him to track down a missing pair of pants. West had sent them out to be pressed during an afternoon break and they had not been returned. West was expected to attend a Dayton Council meeting and needed the pants. Whitehead managed to track down the missing trousers and return them to West in time to get to the meeting.[113]

That same year, the executive board had to consider a name change to reflect the growth of the council to the area outside Dayton. It was proposed to rename the council the Miami Valley Council, but Dayton folk were opposed. A compromise was reached and the name became the Dayton-Miami Valley Council. In later years, the "Dayton" was dropped and the council is now Miami Valley Council.

Also in 1928, Dayton undertook an experiment that was noted by the national council. A troop was formed for physically challenged boys. Each boy was assigned a "buddy," who was a local businessman. The men attended all activities with their buddy and the two advanced through Scouting ranks together. Transportation was provided for the boys to get to meetings and other activities by a businessmen's club. Today, boys with physical problems are accommodated in most troops and all Scout camps. Special provisions are made for them to earn badges while adjusting requirements for their particular situation.

As noted previously, the Third World Jamboree was held at Arrowe Park, Birkenhead, England in 1929. Twenty-five boys and a Scoutmaster from Dayton-Miami Valley made the trip. It was the only U.S. troop made up of boys from a single council. Perle Whitehead was sent along at the expense of the Dayton Rotary Club, with no duties. It was meant to be a well-earned vacation for him. The group went to New York and sailed for England, landing at Liverpool. The ship was full of American Boy Scouts on a huge adventure and it must have been a great time for them all. The Jamboree was the largest gathering of youth in history to that time. 50,000 Scouts from 73 countries were on hand. The boys were treated to visits by British royalty, including the then extremely popular Prince of Wales, who later became King Edward VIII and then Duke of Windsor. Even in those days, trading among boys of various nations was hugely popular, and one of the most sought-after items was the American First Class Badge. It was a large, gold colored representation of the full BSA emblem. The Dayton boys found that they could get almost anything in trade for one of those. It is unlikely that any Scout would have had more than two First Class badges (one was worn on the hat and another on the pocket), so they would have been a rarity.

After the Jamboree, the boys toured London, went to Belgium and Holland and then visited Paris, where they found the Eiffel Tower elevator out of order. Of course, the whole gang climbed to the top and then down again. They also attended the Paris Opera and met a lady opera singer they were quite taken with. It was quite a trip for a bunch of Midwestern boys who had mostly never been out of Ohio.

In 1931, the council took advantage of empty real estate to move offices to a building where they had access to a swimming pool, a gym and an auditorium. Very few council offices have ever had such amenities. Whitehead was a very amiable man and simply would not refuse to see anybody who dropped by to pass the time. Since a lot of men were unemployed or underemployed, there were often visitors just there to chat. The building was only about 20% occupied, so Whitey would take a typewriter, chair and card table and head for one of the vacant offices. Of course, people soon found he was doing this and started tracking him down.

When Perle was in England for the Jamboree, he saw the little British Austin motorcar. He liked it so much, he bought one, but of course the little car and Scout-age boys led to at least one occasion when Perle came out to his parking spot and found the Austin missing. He quickly discovered it up on the steps of the High School, which was right across the street. His reaction can only be imagined, but long-time Scouters know that this kind of thing is usually a sign of affection on the part of the boys, however irritating or inconvenient it may be at times.

It is widely known that the annual Soap Box Derby began in Dayton, and moved a year later to Akron, where it still is held. What is less widely known is that the Derby began as a Boy Scout project. A Scout named Myron Scott got a race going among Scouts and then suggested a city-wide race to the *Dayton Daily News*. The newspaper sponsored a Derby in 1933. Myron Scott went on to work for General Motors where he was able to get the Soap Box Derby sponsored as a nationwide event.[114]

A Regional Camperall was held in Covington, Kentucky in the summer of 1934. Over 2000 Scouts attended from three states. Daniel Carter Beard, "Uncle Dan," was the guest of honor. Boys were awed by this woodsman and pioneer Boy Scout. Beard did not disappoint. He gave boys dried bear meat, showed off woodsy tricks and told stories of pioneer days. He also told stories of his own boyhood, when, at age twelve, he had been an orderly in a hospital during the War Between the States.

That fall, John Yeck, who was an Akron Eagle Scout, joined the professional staff of the council. Yeck had gone to college with a view to professional Scouting as a career, attended National Training School and thus was one of the first in the nation to have planned out a career path from his youth. He had been influenced by his Scout Executive, Dwight Ramsey, who would later serve as Region Four Executive and then on the staff of the national personnel division. Yeck had many talents, including radio. He and others produced a serial weekly on a local radio stations about the adventures of "Captain Stormalong," with characters portrayed by Yeck and his friends, mainly Scouts and Scouters.

In 1936, Perle Whitehead was asked to move up to become Deputy Regional Executive of Region Four, and a huge farewell was held for him prior to his departure. He was succeeded by B.W. Stayton as Scout Executive.

Cub Scouting had been around for about ten years, but had attracted little interest, in Dayton or elsewhere for that matter. In Dayton the program was run like Boy Scouting with scaled down activities. The younger boys didn't do well and many were turned off on the whole idea of being a Scout, just the opposite of what the program was meant to do.

New methods had been developed and were being taught at the National Training School, so Stayton got Charles A. Whitcomb, who joined the staff in 1937, to take on the Cub Scout program in the council.

His first job was to kill off Cub Scouting as it existed and start it anew with the current methods.

This involved careful negotiations with parents and those who sponsored the Cub Scout Packs. Training had to be instituted for the new "Den Mothers" who would lead small groups of Cubs. Packs would now meet monthly with parents in attendance and dens would meet weekly, usually at a Den Mother's home. Somehow, they pulled it off and the Cub Scout program became a major supplier of recruits for Scouting nationwide.[115] In recent years, BSA has changed the Cub program once again, so that it resembles in many ways (at least for ten and eleven year old boys) the old program and the result has been much the same as it was in the 1930s.

World War II affected Dayton-Miami Valley like other Scout councils around the country. Scouts were involved in war work and professionals and volunteers went off to war. Also like other places, Scouts in Dayton offered whatever they could to help out Scouts overseas in the aftermath of the war. They had a special "shirt off my back" campaign to get Scouts to donate.

Lieutenant General Nathan F. Twining, then commanding the Air Technical Service Command (later renamed Air Materiel Command) at Wright-Patterson Air Force Base, offered up the shirt off his back to the unit that collected the most donations.

In 1948, the council was selected to test an ill-conceived program idea. It was decided to combine all the older boy programs into one, comprised of Sea Scouts, Air Scouts and Explorers. It didn't work and the programs were separated again, although Air Scouting was eventually allowed to die out, to the regret of many former Air Scouts. In recent years, the BSA has found a more successful way of doing this. There is a program called Learning for Life, which allows youth over 14 to become involved in vocational work, including aviation. Especially popular are the police and fire career programs, sometimes still referred to as Police Explorers and Fire Explorers.

The BSA Venturing program also encompasses boys and girls age fourteen through twenty. Boys may choose to remain in Scout troops until age eighteen if they wish and some participate in both programs.

Venturing has one specialty within it, called Sea Scouting. Sea Scouts have their own advancement program, leading to the Quartermaster Award, considered by some to be more prestigious than Eagle Scout.

Other Venturing units may choose their own specialty, whether high adventure, camping or almost any other pursuit they like. There are Venturing awards available to them, as well.

In 1966, the Golden Anniversary of Miami Valley Council was marked by a recognition dinner that was attended by Perle Whitehead and two of the old-time Scoutmasters, George Clark, who was Whitehead's "replacement" as Scoutmaster and A.W. Payne, who had led Troop 30 since 1919.

Dwight Ramsey

Camp Manatoc and the Spell of Marnoc

Dwight Ramsey was born in 1894 in Salem, Indiana. After college he became principal of an elementary school in Decatur, Illinois. Dwight registered as a Scoutmaster in 1916 and became interested in joining as a professional.

He became a professional Scouter in 1917 in Elgin, Illinois, but within months he joined the Army. Dwight went to officer training and was commissioned a Second Lieutenant. He was released from the Army in December, 1918, at the end of World War I.

He returned to professional Scouting, first as a District Scout Executive in Chicago and then, in 1920, as Scout Executive in Akron, Ohio. When he arrived, Akron did not have a council camp. The Scouts had been holding summer camp in a number of unsatisfactory locations.

A committee was set up to study locations and visit existing Scout camps to assess what was needed for an ideal camp. As committees will, the men studied the situation, and drew up a list of requirements for an ideal camp. A dinner was hosted by one of the members and key civic leaders of Akron were in attendance.

Ramsey thought that the men would start volunteering to get the real work underway, but the report was made after dinner, the committee was congratulated, and everyone went home. Ramsey had just learned a valuable lesson in the work of a Scout Executive. He had failed to make the desired result happen.

As it turned out, one of the attendees ran into his old school friend, Karl Butler, a few days later and mentioned the meeting. Butler was a businessman in Akron with an interesting history who loved camping and was interested in Scouting. Butler suggested that they consider using a 200-acre parcel he owned, explaining that Scouts had been using the land as a camping and hiking spot.

Ramsey and the committee visited the land and immediately saw difficulties. The land was hilly and only a plateau between two ridges would be usable as a camp. A test well did not find a convenient water supply.

Butler remained certain that it could be made to work and in 1922 the committee decided to build a camp there, leasing the land from Butler. A surveyor was hired to map the land. Decisions had to be made about buildings, a swimming place, water source and lines, drainage, latrines and many other factors.

It was apparent that they would need more land. So Butler and Ramsey began talking to owners of adjacent parcels. Most agreed, under various conditions, to allow use of parts of their land.

Next on the agenda, and ultimately most important, was funding. Ramsey talked to several groups around town. The Better Akron Federation, a group established to help during World War I, consolidated a number of other groups and acted as a sort of United Way. The Federation was willing to allow the council to hold a capital campaign to raise $6,125.

Over the years between 1925 and 1931, the Federation also gave the council over $223,000 in grants. Most of the civic clubs and organizations in Akron donated money, materials or labor to the construction of the camp.

Construction began in 1923, with the building of a road. Mules were used to level and grade the switch-backed road into camp. The road was later used only to get supplies into camp. Visitors parked and walked in. A cable was also run from the top of the hill so that supplies could be placed in an attached container and let down into camp.

There was a creek, Haskell Run, through one of the ravines. A dam was built at one end to create a swimming area. The ravine had to be cleared of trees, stumps and debris to make a safe swimming hole. Somehow, however, a large snapping turtle ended up in the lake when it was filled and boys got mysterious, minor bites while swimming all summer. The turtle was discovered when the lake was allowed to drain at the end of the first camping season.

Three buildings were to be built: a dining hall, administrative building and an assembly hall. The buildings were raised above ground by means of sewer pipes filled with concrete, which were available at no cost from Butler's family business. Electric lines were run, a deep well was drilled and water lines were laid. A water tower was built near the well at the highest point in camp, so that water pressure would not be a problem.

In June, 1923, the camp opened for its first summer. Facilities were incomplete and construction was still underway during camp. Campers were assigned to eight boy tents with a cot for each and four storage boxes for gear. A kerosene lantern, a big no-no in today's Scouting because of fire safety concerns, was in each tent.

Boys in those days generally did not have sleeping bags so used blankets for cover, with their laundry bag as a pillow. At one time, blanket pins like large safety pins were sold as an item in the BSA National Supply Service catalog. In the early days, no cold drinks were sold in camp, so a popular spot was the drinking fountain at the assembly hall, where ice would be placed around the pipe when it was available.

The camp had to have a name, so Ramsey asked an older Scout, David Atwater, to do some research and come up with a suitable one. David found the Indian word, "Manatoc," which meant a high place where councils are held.

Atwater also wrote a very inspiring closing ceremony. A poem, actually, called "The Spell of Marnoc." It described the search of a brave for a restless spirit dwelling in a cave. This spirit, Marnoc, supposedly was present at Camp Manatoc. Reading the poem, it is easy to imagine a group of boys sitting spellbound around a campfire listening to it.

Karl Butler loved to camp at Manatoc and would set up a tent near the dining hall where he would stay at times during camp. Butler suffered from a tubercular arthritis disease that caused extreme curvature of the spine. In those days, he would have been called a hunchback. He was obviously able to get around fairly well, but needed help at times. He enjoyed camping and would talk to any boys who wanted to chat.

Camp activities were pretty similar to those of most camps, but one feature was almost certainly unique to Manatoc. For several summers in the 1920s, Goodyear Tire and Rubber Company would send blimps out to camp and each boy got to ride in the passenger compartment for a flight around camp. At a time when few boys had flown in airplanes, this must have been an exciting adventure.

Over the years, Karl Butler purchased additional land adjacent to the camp whenever it was available. In late 1926, Karl was taken ill. He realized how serious his condition was and called in the council office secretary to take down a last will and testament. He died a day or two later.

In his will, Butler left all of his property to the Akron Area Council. There was a provision that the council had to raise $100,000, in order to purchase more adjoining land, over five years, in which case the cost of the land would be one dollar for 414 acres.

A large funeral was held at which Dwight Ramsey served as a pallbearer. In August, a memorial service was held at Camp Manatoc. A great deal of preparation went into it, because a large crowd was expected and facilities at camp were not adequate. As it happened, an estimated 3000 people came to the service.

With the additional money and acreage, Camp Manatoc was rebuilt on another part of the property. However, parts of the old camp, now remote and seldom visited, are still visible. Some of the concrete-filled sewer pipes still stand and there is evidence of the old road. Some know where they are and occasionally visit the nostalgic old site.[116]

Dwight Ramsey moved on in 1931. He became Regional Executive of Region Four and then Region Seven. In the late Thirties, he went to the national office and was chief instructor for Council Organization and Administration for the National Training School at Schiff Scout Reservation. In 1951, he became Regional Executive for Region Two. He retired in 1959.[117]

P.V. Thorson

New Mexico Professional and Alligator Tamer

P.V. Thorson was an almost-from-the-beginning Scouter. Born in 1898, he joined Scouting in Kansas City in 1911 and was part of a troop there for five years. When he moved to Santa Fe, New Mexico in 1919, he started a troop and served as Scoutmaster until 1921. He left Santa Fe to enroll at the University of New Mexico in 1921 and in 1925 joined the ranks of professionals as Scout Executive of the Albuquerque Council.

Thorson began working as a part time, paid executive and meantime worked part time as a coal company clerk. During his tenure, Thorson was part of a six-week training course at the University of New Mexico, for credit, at a cost of $2.50 per enrollee. Dr. West visited during the course and pronounced himself satisfied. Whether the course had any effect on the national training school that began about the same time is not known, but it would be safe to assume it may have.

Thorson also recruited a Mr. Otero to work directly with boys of Hispanic descent, which was very successful. Thorson and two others were invited to speak, through a translator, at a school for primarily Hispanic students. During the talk, enough snow fell to make a return journey impossible for the night, so Thorson and the others were invited to spend the night with a local family. They were fed and entertained, but the family would not go to bed as the evening grew later and later. At last something was said and the group was informed the family members were waiting for them to retire as they were given the home's only bedroom and the family was to sleep in the living room.

Thorson got himself in trouble and made history at the same time during a visit to a former Scout Executive in Orange, Texas. The conversation somehow turned to alligators and P.V. said facetiously that he would love to have one for his council. The other man actually sent him one and it was delivered to the Scout office in a box. Thorson left the critter in the office overnight thinking it would be safe enough, but the gator managed to escape and early next morning Thorson got a panicked call from his secretary. Thorson rushed to the office and somehow got the reptile back in its crate, in which it was soon delivered to the Albuquerque Zoo. They were the first, and possibly only, council ever to donate a live alligator to a zoo.

Another member joined the council staff in an unusual way. Mr. Benjamin Talbot Babbit "Uncle Benny" Hyde was a naturalist and member of several organizations such as the Explorers Club in New York It seems he was at the American Museum of Natural History in New York, trying to discover what would provoke a rattlesnake to bite. As a result, the small rattler bit him, putting venom directly into a blood vein. It almost killed him and the doctors recommended he go to New Mexico to recover his health. Uncle Benny had been a National Field Commissioner and written portions of the Boy Scout handbook involving nature. He visited Thorson in Albuquerque and as a result he became a member of the professional staff.

In 1931, Thorson resigned to become Scout Executive of the Eastern New Mexico Council at

Roswell, where he succeeded Minor S. Huffman. Then Thorson became Assistant Scout Executive at Houston, Texas and in 1944 became Scout Executive of the Buffalo Trail Council at Sweetwater, Texas. In 1963, he retired from professional Scouting and moved back to Albuquerque, where he served as a volunteer. In 1982, he was called upon to write the history of what was then the Great Southwest Council in Albuquerque. Several stories in that history are of interest.[118]

There was a Scout troop at Raton, in northeastern New Mexico in 1914 that went on a two week camping adventure around the mountainous areas of that part of New Mexico. The boys took a train from Raton to Ute Park, where they camped for 10 days. They then hiked over the mountains to the Urraca Creek drainage area and down to Cimarron, New Mexico. There was a ranch there owned by a George Webster, who provided hospitality for the Scouts and allowed them to camp on the ranch. According to Thorson, the Webster home later became the site of Philmont Scout Ranch Camping Headquarters, making that group the first Scouts ever to camp at Philmont, over 25 years before it became a Scouting facility.[119]

According to Thorson, the council was visited at one time by legendary Sea Scout National Director, Commander Thomas Keane. Keane expressed some surprise at the number of Sea Scout units in existence in the council. He asked Thorson where the Sea Scouts sailed and Thorson replied, "We sail prairie schooners on heat waves."[120] Keane was probably afraid to ask any more questions about the subject. It has been apparent over the years that Sea Scouting is just as popular in dry places as in those surrounded by water. In the State of Hawaii in 2007, there was only one Sea Scout unit. A lot of Navy people come from those dry parts of the country as well.

It seems that odd things happened wherever Thorson went. In 1937, a large man aged 55 or 60 years appeared at the council office in Roswell. He wore a fringed buckskin shirt, cowboy boots and a frontier style hat. He introduced himself to Thorson as Kit Carson, a nephew of the original, who had lived in New Mexico (and had a home on what is now Philmont Scout Ranch). Thorson invited Carson to be a part of an upcoming Council Camporee. Between the two of them, they cooked up a stagecoach and an Indian raid to take place during the camporee. According to Thorson, it "added greatly to the success of the Camp-o-ree."[121]

Thorson was also responsible for the *Ripley's Believe It or Not* newspaper coverage of Boy Scouts visiting the Carlsbad Caverns in 1940.[122] Unfortunately, the author has been unable to find any more of Thorson's exploits following his departure from the Eastern New Mexico Council in 1944.

M.H.F. Kinsey
Hiker and Outdoorsman

The full name of Mr. Kinsey was Macon Hereford Flowerree Kinsey, which probably explains the fact that he never used anything other than the three initials.[123] He was always known as M.H.F. Kinsey. He was, in any event, the first Scout Executive of the Buckskin Council of West Virginia (then the Charleston Area Council). Kinsey went to work for the YMCA in Richmond in 1911 and went to Portsmouth, Ohio sometime later. From his work, he concluded that to accomplish anything with boys, a man must be interested in the same things they are. This echoes what was said earlier about "boy-men."

We don't know how Kinsey found Scouting, but we do know that he organized boys from the "Y" into the first Boy Scout Troop in Portsmouth. He organized more troops and became the first Scout Executive in Portsmouth in 1911. In that year, there were fewer than a dozen Scout Executives in the country.[124] He left Ohio to become Scout Executive in Kalamazoo, Michigan in 1918, but he didn't stay there long. He and his family suffered ill health in the cold winters and, a year later, he moved to Charleston.

As part of the hiring process, he was asked to give a presentation to the entire council committee, with two hours notice. He chose "Dollars or boys?" as his topic, emphasizing that in the modern search for wealth, the really important values are overlooked. An interesting topic, given that much of a Scout Executive's job has to do with raising money. He was hired and soon living in Charleston.

Kinsey was an avid hiker and outdoorsman and started an organization, the Appalachian Trailblazers, which survived for 20 years. It was open to non-Scouts and they regularly took 20 mile hikes around the area. He even created a series of award emblems that could be worn by those completing 100 and up to 1000 miles of hiking.[125]

Kinsey saw that one of the first needs for the council was to have its own Scout camp. After some searching a site was found and leased.

Camp Pequoni, which opened in 1920, was a long way from town and accessible only by rail, but they made it work for a number of years. Fortunately, there were no serious medical emergencies at camp, but one incident dramatized the problem.

A local woman came into camp one morning, having been bitten by a poisonous copperhead snake. An Eagle Scout in camp made an incision with a razor blade, bandaged her arm and somehow convinced a railroad section gang to lend them a handcar (a device like a platform with railcar wheels that sits on railroad tracks, with locomotion provided by pumping a seesaw handle), which they used to transport the lady to the next town, where there was a doctor. Luckily, the copperhead is the least venomous poisonous snake in the U.S. and the lady survived. The treatment she received was probably standard for the time, but not recommended today.

Practice mobilizations were part of the program for Scouts in the Charleston area. Kinsey's assistant Scout Executive, Emmit Thaxton, designed a code system which would quickly be passed from Scout to Scout. The code was a set of numbers such as, 1489-630. The first digit was assembly location, the second, third and fourth would be equipment needed by the Scout and the final group of digits, the time of assembly.

These practice mobilizations became real on several occasions. In April, 1928, boys were assembled to fight forest fires. Sixty boys, along with their leaders, were transported 25 miles to the site. The call came in at 11 a.m. Such was the level of confidence in the Boy Scouts of Charleston that the Forestry Service called Kinsey directly to ask if he could get some Scouts out to a couple of serious fires. The boys were on site to fight fires by 3 p.m. This in a time when many people still had no telephone. The Scouts fought the fires under supervision of forest rangers, with appropriate rest periods, until dawn the next day. Much property and many homes were saved by these boys. Not coincidentally, we are told that many of the same boys went on to become successful men who contributed much to their community.

Yet another successful mobilization occurred when the State Capitol building burned. Kinsey happened on the scene in the afternoon, to discover Scoutmasters had mobilized boys who were busy removing state records from the building. Kinsey went back to his office and contacted the schools to get more Scouts excused for the job. Many records were saved by the Scouts on that day, apparently without injury to any of them. Actions like this had a significant impact on the regard people of the community held for Scouting.

It was soon decided that the council needed a better located camping area and one was soon found. The Scout Executive and the Council President drafted an option to purchase the land on their first visit. A survey was done and everyone was ready to close on the given date and time. The option expired at noon, but the concerned men got stuck on a muddy road and had to work for about an hour to free the vehicle. They arrived at the seller's home at 11:45 a.m. and got all the documents signed. The seller pointed out that the option called for a $1000, which would amount to about $13,000 in 2012, payment on delivery of the deed and annual payments of the same amount thereafter. Somehow, Kinsey had overlooked this factor. He had not brought a council check and also knew there were not sufficient funds in the account to cover it. So, without batting an eye, Kinsey wrote a personal check for the thousand dollars, knowing he also didn't have that much in his account. First thing next morning, he visited the finance committee chairman for the council and explained the situation. The man gave Kinsey a personal check for $750.00, which would bring the council balance up to the right level. Kinsey then deposited the money and got a council check payable to him which prevented an overdraft. Excitement has always been part of professional Scouting. Camp Walhonde became the new council camp.[126]

A telegram was received by Kinsey one day in his office. It was from the camp director at Camp Walhonde, saying, "Rush ambulance and doctor, two boys drowned." Kinsey later said the incident turned his hair grey overnight.[127] Since there were no phones at camp, nothing could be known until they got there. Camp wasn't yet open for the summer, but the staff was setting up camp. All were known to be good swimmers.

Arriving at camp, they found a group huddled around a wagon on which there was a boy's body. The doctor who went with Kinsey to the camp quickly determined he was beyond saving and that the boys were not Scouts. It developed that a Sunday school class with their teacher had come by, asking to use the camp swimming hole on the river. The director explained no one was allowed to use it unless lifeguards were present.

The teacher and the boys went upriver away from the camp and two boys went in. They got into trouble and since the teacher was unable to swim, they sank. Camp staff were called in and managed to get one of the boys out and start artificial respiration. They continued for over an hour, but were not able to revive him. The body of the other boy was not recovered until after Kinsey arrived.

Kinsey was wise enough to realize that there could be confusion in the minds of the public, since the incident was near the camp, and hurried back to Charleston. He conferred with the city editors of both local newspapers and made sure they understood what had happened. The whole incident served to contrast the preparedness and safety concerns of the Scouts with the irresponsibility of the Sunday school teacher who let his boys drown. In some ways, things never change. It is an often overlooked point even today that it is essential to get the facts of the story straight in minds of the media before anything gets to the airwaves. Of course, in our communication-rich environment, it is far more difficult than just talking to the city editors. A couple of years ago, when a tornado touched down in Scout summer camp, resulting in injuries and deaths, cell phone photos were on the internet within an hour or two.

As council histories always show, camping needs change as demographics and membership numbers do. In 1945, a long-time Scouter donated a new camp of over one hundred acres to the Council. The camp had some buildings already in place. Council members decided to sell Camp Walhonde and move to Camp Clifton McClintic. The old camp was sold. Camp McClintic was also outgrown in a fairly short time and Buckskin Reservation, a six hundred acre tract opened in 1960. This is still the main Scout Camp for Buckskin Council.

The Great Depression hit Charleston, as it did other councils. Kinsey was forced to lay off his assistant, his full-time secretary and take a 15 per cent pay cut to survive.

The Second World War soon followed, taking many volunteers to war. Kinsey went out to older former Scoutmasters to take the place of the ones serving in the military. Having been a Scout Executive in World War I, Kinsey was quick to mobilize Scouts and Scouters to assist in the war effort. In fact, a letter went out to Scoutmasters on December 10, 1941, only 2 days after war was declared. As in other places, the Scouts collected scrap paper, aluminum and performed other services vital to the war effort.

Baden-Powell had in mind a program that would instill certain principles and values in young boys as a foundation for good citizenship so that they would view themselves as valued members of a community and nation. That view has remained constant in a changing world.

Mr. Kinsey retired in1947 and remains the longest serving Scout Executive in council history. Nothing could be found about his later days or death. Interestingly, however, Kinsey was the author of a tune, *Boy Scout March*, which can still be found, and a book, *The Treasure of Lost Cave, a Boy Scout Story,* copyrighted in 1921.

The BSA has recently obtained a major tract of land in the middle of Buckskin Council. The Summit Bechtel Reserve, better known as "The Summit," will be home to the next National Jamboree in 2013, and a World Jamboree in 2019. At this time, it is planned to hold all future U.S. Jamborees at the Summit. In addition, there are facilities being built there for a national high adventure base which will operate year around for Scouts.

G.H. Oberteuffer

Camp Meriwether, Portland Oregon

Yet one more long-serving Scout Executive, G.H. "Obie" Oberteuffer headed the council in Portland, Oregon from 1925 to 1957. He had an incredible career in professional Scouting, having served as a Boy Scout camp director while he was teaching in a high school, Scout Executive in Spokane and then as Regional Scout Executive of Region Eleven of the BSA.

Not much historical information is available on these early parts of his career, but his work as Scout Executive in Portland is lovingly detailed in a little history written by a man named Kenneth Wells, who met Oberteuffer as a boy and later was mentored by him.[128]

James E. Brockway, the Scout Executive in Portland, resigned to take a position with *Boys Life* magazine in New York. There was an immediate controversy that arose out of the fact that Brockway had seen the officially established advancement requirements as minimums and had added a great many requirements that existed only in that council.

For instance, he required that a boy be able to send and receive in both semaphore and Morse code to earn his First Class badge. National required only one or the other. A boy also had to build a fire by friction and craft a bow and arrow that would shoot 75 yards. These were not part of national requirements, which were published in every Scout handbook. As a result of these requirements, very few boys ever achieved First Class rank, which meant there were very few Eagle Scouts in the council and those who had achieved that goal were held in very high esteem.[129]

When Oberteuffer arrived, he immediately did away with these extra requirements, as was correct. Today there is an express prohibition against adding to any badge requirements. While this was a big relief to younger boys beginning the Scout advancement trail, it was a disappointment to the few Eagle Scouts who had struggled through Brockway's standards and made the grade.

Kenneth Wells was one of these. He was Senior Patrol Leader of his troop and he and some other boys decided to have an open debate on the issue. Parents and outsiders were invited and Oberteuffer was invited to join the debate. He immediately accepted. Wells led for the proposition that these changes were degrading to the program and the judges, a panel of parents and leaders, decided that his side won. Obie graciously accepted defeat, although he didn't return to the old requirements, and went up and offered Wells a job on the summer camp staff.

The summer camp was located on leased land and called Camp Chinidere. As luck would have it, the camp lodge burned to the ground near the end of the camping season.

This camp was located in such a way that a 14 mile trek on foot was needed to get into or out of it, quite a drawback for getting supplies in and out, not to mention visitors. Obie got $6000, a large sum in those days, from the insurance company and decided the council should look for a different property that it could own outright.

He found one, but there were some problems. It was located a long way from town by the standards of the day, there were no roads leading to it and the final price was $24,000! Of course, there were offsetting advantages: it was a beautiful piece of land on a bluff over the Pacific Ocean and they were able to get 500 acres. Few, if any, councils in the country could foresee a time when they would need that much land for a council camp. Obie could, and Camp Meriwether was born. The camp name was derived from Meriwether Lewis, of the Lewis and Clark expedition.

The main parcel of the property had been a farm owned by people named Chamberlain and had an interesting history. In 1890, a derelict Norwegian schooner, the *Struan*, came ashore at the foot of the property. The local newspaper at the time had said it came ashore at "an inconvenient place," and many who inspected the site at the time of purchase had the same thought.

All building material had to be carried in to the camp sites Obie had selected. These sites were widely separated and tents were to be placed on platforms built up on hillsides. Years later, after the tents, which had been salvaged from Camp Chinidere, were no longer usable, the platforms were shingled over and converted into cabins.

A dining hall and the troop sites were constructed in 1926. The workers, mostly volunteers, were under a lot of pressure to get the camp ready for its opening in June of that year. Most operations that would normally take place in buildings had to operate out of tents in the first year.

The dining hall itself was kind of a thrown-together affair. It had no windows for the first couple of years and the kitchen was a separate building with no covered connection between the two. The reason, of course, was the thought of another fire. Unfortunately, it also meant the boys carrying the food into the dining hall and the dishes out got soaked whenever it rained.

When opening day came, the dining hall was only half roofed and the dining tables had not yet arrived. The campers therefore had the opportunity to eat their meals standing for a couple of weeks until the tables came in. Camp Meriwether did open, with fanfare, on the scheduled date and everybody made do as things gradually got more organized.

Obie's biographer, Ken Wells, worked for a number of years at camp. He tells a couple of stories about the man in his writings. One such was an occasion when the two drove around Portland on some errands in Oberteuffer's Model T Ford to obtain some supplies. They reached the council office building on a main street and Obie got out and told the teenager to park the car and bring in the keys. He never asked the young man whether he'd ever driven before. He hadn't, but had watched Obie driving enough to know what the pedals did and how to shift gears. After a stall or two–luckily, the coupe was equipped with an electric starter, so no hand cranking was needed–he found a spot where he could pull straight forward to the curb and stop. He had no idea how to back up. He took the keys to Obie and it was only after they finished their business at the office and returned to the car that Obie thought to ask Wells if he had ever driven before.

Oberteuffer was very interested in Senior Scouting, which was a new program idea. It was designed as a way for older teens to do some things without the younger boys slowing them down. Sea Scouting, which had been around since 1912 and was also for older teens, flourished and for quite some years, Portland had more Sea Scouts than any council in the U.S. Portland ships frequently were designated Regional and National Flagships in those years.[130]

Obie retired with a special Scouter's weekend held, appropriately, at Camp Meriwether in May of 1957, after 32 years of service. Scout executives today rarely get to spend more than four or five years at a council before they are moved elsewhere for career reasons. Sometimes, that can be a very good thing, but the impact of one man on a particular council and its camping facilities over a long period can be wonderful if he is the right man at the right time. Obie Oberteuffer would certainly be such a man.

Under Oberteuffer, the council purchased land in 1949 and constructed a camp on Spirit Lake, on the slopes of Mount St. Helens, a long-dormant volcano which began to show signs of becoming active in 1980. The council managed to get a good deal of equipment out by cargo helicopter before the mountain blew, but the camp itself (and Spirit Lake) was destroyed for all time that year when the volcano erupted, an event which captured the attention of all Americans.[131]

H.S. Alvord

International Jamboree at Independence Rock, Wyoming

In 1924, Scouting had been well established in Bonneville and Jefferson counties of Idaho. A National Field Commissioner, a Mr. Freeman, arrived to encourage the communities to form a council and hire a Scout Executive.

H.S. Alvord had been a school teacher in Logan, Utah, and had attended a Scout Executives National Council School held at Estes Park, Colorado. He seemed the right man for the job and was hired as Scout Executive of what shortly became the Teton Peaks Council, which today serves eastern Idaho, western Wyoming, and West Yellowstone, Montana

The only information available today comes from a book, or really a pamphlet, authored by Willard Adams. Adams was in Scouting from 1916 until at least 1951. We know he was born in 1898 and died in 1988 and that he was a member of the Church of Jesus Christ of Latter Day Saints, or Mormon. He held many Scouting positions, including Scoutmaster and received one of the first Silver Beavers in the Teton Peaks Council.[132]

A group from the council was selected to attend what was called International Jamboree, not to be confused with the World Jamborees which had been held in Europe, at Independence Rock between July 3 and July 5, 1930. The rock is a famous landmark on the old Oregon Trail in Wyoming that had been established 100 years before. Details of how the event came about are sketchy, but Chief Scout Executive James E. West was in attendance, along with the Governor of Wyoming and other dignitaries, as were about 1200 Scouts and Scouters. There were speeches, commemorative dedications, an Indian pageant put on by 25 members of the Shoshone tribe, fireworks and a lot of Scout fellowship.

In 1936, Alvord left to become Scout Executive in Omaha, Nebraska and was replaced by Vernon L. Strong, a local man who had been a Scoutmaster and then became a professional. He had been serving as Scout Executive in Eureka, California. Strong served the council at least until 1951, which is approximately the date of Adams' book.

R.R. Adcock

Clyde Barrow's Probation Officer

R.R. Adcock served as Council Commissioner and then Scout Executive of the Sam Houston Area Council sometime just after 1915. He had been a Scoutmaster and remained active as a professional Scouter into the 1930s. He was also camp director at Camp Masterson and other camps during that era.

Prior to his involvement in Scouting, R. R., (no other names can be found for him, although some of his friends called him "Rube," so perhaps he was Ruben), Adcock had been in law enforcement. He was also called "General" because of his uniforming and his strong belief in discipline.

His picture shows a handsome man wearing a tailored uniform and a perfectly straight-brimmed "Smokey Bear" hat.[133]

He is included here because prior to his service as a professional Scouter R.R. had been a probation officer in Harris County, Texas. There in 1918 one of his "clients" was 8-year-old Clyde Barrow, who later became quite famous, along with his girlfriend Bonnie Parker, as Bonnie and Clyde.[134]

The Men of Delaware and Montgomery County Council, PA

A Sesquicentennial Exposition and a National Meeting in 1926

In 1927, the Delaware and Montgomery Counties Council of Pennsylvania published the *1926 Annual*, a book of council activities from that year, which is the only council history found to date. The council later became Valley Forge Council and eventually merged with the Cradle of Liberty Council, headquartered in Philadelphia.[135]

There is a photo of all the men on the executive staff of the council, taken at Valley Forge. The names are:

Wilmer H. Brown
E.N. Weikel
Russell Moll
Henry M. Faucett
Edward A. Carson (Scout Executive)
Chester L. Nelson
Raymond Boxworth
George M. Stewart
John R. Porter
James M. Hart

The council had an interesting year in 1926. The highlight of that year was a trip to Washington DC for two train-car loads of Scouts and men from the council. The purpose of the trip was to greet the Founder of Scouting, Sir Robert Baden-Powell, who was accompanied by his young wife, Olave, Lady Baden-Powell. A White House event was laid on for the British visitors and the roster of attendees included Dan Beard and all the top men of the BSA, along with the Pennsylvania Scouts. The President, Calvin Coolidge, was on hand to greet all the guests. Unfortunately, the details of the event were not included in the Annual and probably were less significant to the Scouts than touring the capitol. We know, however, that B-P and President Coolidge attended the meeting of the National Council of the Boy Scouts of America at which he was presented the first Silver Buffalo, BSA's highest award. The second Silver Buffalo went to the unknown Scout who, in BSA legend, met William Boyce in London over 20 years earlier. It was represented by a statue of a Silver Buffalo which still stands at Gilwell Park, British Scouting's outdoor center, outside London.[136]

Also during the trip, the Pennsylvania Scouts were given the singular opportunity to hold a religious service in the Amphitheater in Arlington Cemetery. Following the service, the Scouts gathered at the Tomb of the Unknown Soldier, then brand new and still without its distinctive decorative marble cap, and one of the boys played Taps. This was before the time of the perpetual military guard of honor at the Tomb.

Boys and men from the council also participated in a Sesquicentennial International Exposition in Philadelphia. The National Council had gone all out for the event and put up a Scout booth, called The Scoutcraft Trail. An artist had painted a mural, portraying medieval knights evolving into Boy Scouts as a background and lettered the Scout Oath and the Scout Law on the wall next to it. Scouts, including the ones from Delaware and Montgomery Counties, manned the booth during the five-month event. Mr. Carson, the Scout Executive, worked on the exhibit committee with E. Urner Goodman, who was at the time Scout Executive of the Philadelphia Council. Among the thousands of visitors to the Exposition were leaders and boys from a number of foreign countries, including China and Japan. Although the exposition itself was a financial disaster for the promoters, it must have been very exciting for the boy participants from Pennsylvania.[137]

The Council also sent a delegation of two men and one of their wives to the Eastern States Exposition at Springfield, Massachusetts in 1926.

The Exposition, which is still an annual event in Springfield, featured quite a sizeable contingent of Boy Scouts and leaders, who lived in wigwams in a Native American village. There were typical Scouting skills being demonstrated and a section of merit badge booths, where visitors could participate in skills like archery and basket weaving.

An interesting project of the council that year was an extension program to support a Scout troop in Labrador. Only nine boys were in the troop, which was located in a remote part of a remote land. The council furnished them with uniforms, neckerchiefs, badges and Scout handbooks. Everything had to be shipped in by Fall, because the mail boat couldn't reach them again until spring thaw. It must have been interesting for these boys who lived in a British Dominion to use American Scout books and adapt their Oath and Law to conform to their national loyalties.

The Railway Executives
Traveling Organizers on the Rails in the Southwest

A nearly forgotten chapter in the saga of early Scouting in the Southwest was the work of the railway executives. It seems that vandalism to railway property in many communities was the work of boys who otherwise had nothing to do with their time. The railroads had heard of Scouting and its principles and decided it might well be to their advantage to organize troops in the communities along their lines. As it happened, it was to everyone's advantage.

After meeting with regional officials and the concurrence of the national office, the main railroads began to hire men approved by the BSA to serve as organizers of Scout units. The men carried the title of National Field Scout Executive and were part of each line's safety department.[138] These men would travel the lines of a particular railroad and stop off at towns where they could get to know people, find organizations who would sponsor Scouting and recruit men and boys to form units. The same men trained the initial leadership. In 1927, the Missouri-Kansas-Texas Railroad, the Southern Pacific Railroad and the Missouri Pacific all had railway executives.[139] Some of the men who served in these jobs were O. J. Williams, George Simpson, E.J. Strathern, W.A. Zischang (or Zeschang), Charles A. Knouse and A. F. Sawyer.[140]

Troops formed by these men became part of the local council that served the area.

The program only lasted until about 1930 (the Missouri Pacific kept on until at least 1938), when presumably the job was pretty much done. The Missouri Pacific System issued a statement in 1927 that said, in part, "The success of the Scout work promoted by the railroad has surpassed the fondest expectations of all those interested. Depot agents [on these lines where Scouting was organized] reported a noticeable decrease in vandalism and trespassing of boys on railroad property."[141] A worthy tribute to what can happen when boys are given something to do with their time and are encouraged to follow principles such as the Scout Oath and Law.

The Secretaries

The Men Came and Went – The Ladies Stayed and Kept it Going

Secretaries have been mentioned in this account, and the part they played, particularly in the early days, can't be overemphasized. They were underpaid, overworked and often ran the whole council single-handed when the lone professional was at camp or on the road. In the days of few telephones and no cell phones the men could be out of contact and decisions had to be made.

There are many examples, but one is stands out in council histories. In the 1970s, in the Lebanon County (PA) Council, BSA, there was an abrupt transition, leaving the council without its Scout Executive. The history of that council speaks of Catherine Murray.

With the departure of the Scout Executive, Leo Gruss, Deputy Region Three Scout Executive, acted in this capacity for the [c]ouncil with Field Scout Executive Jim Easterly on the scene in the local office. Miss Catherine Murray was the levening [sic] for the [c]ouncil and kept all affairs in order. She was now in her 43rd year as office secretary, and it later was said that she could have applied to almost any other employer in Lebanon, and she would have been hired, certainly at many times the salary she drew from the Scout Council. But Miss Murray had found her niche in life. Service. Service through Scouting. Her extra-dimensional service, love, dedication, honor and trust are attributes that cannot be purchased. They emanate from within.[142]

From 1927 to at least 1971, this lady was on the job every day and is no doubt typical of many who did the same.

The Camp Rangers
Keepers of the Camps

After a little thought, I realized I would be remiss in omitting camp rangers from this history. A camp ranger is the person who lives at the Scout camp, sometimes in a wonderful home, sometimes in much less, and ensures that the camp doesn't burn down, get vandalized or worse. The ranger's house is usually the first building you see entering a Scout camp. They also are responsible for day-to-day work to keep the camp facilities in good shape. They don't run the camp and usually get a lot of volunteer help with major repairs and clean-ups. The Order of the Arrow usually does a work day or two at camp each year.

However, the ranger controls access to the camp when there is no staff present. Some councils now have a "campmaster" program where volunteers come out on weekends to supervise troops camping there and activities that happen on those weekends. Many camps, where the climate permits, have a camp director who lives on the camp all year and takes care of program. Otherwise, these tasks fall to the ranger.

In most cases, camp rangers are non-professional employees of the BSA. Some are retired professionals, but occasionally a professional Scouter is "offered" the "opportunity" to be camp ranger in his or her spare time. I have known a couple of these professional rangers and it is not an easy life.

An early, close friend of mine in Scouting was Austin "Ike" Sutton. Ike was hired to be a District Executive in the Thunderbird District of the Gulf Ridge Council, Tampa, Florida. He also agreed to live at the suburban Camp Owen Brorein. It's a lovely camp on a small lake with homes and docks all around. It's also very old, dating back to the 1920s. It's now pretty much in the suburbs, but originally it had been way out of town.

Ike had retired from the Air Force, where I met him, and then moved with his family to a little cinder-block house at Camp Brorein. He and Barbara, his wife, had three sons from preteen to teen and one preteen daughter. They also had two large, beautiful Boxers who lived inside. I visited them many times and they never seemed overcrowded, but recently I made a pilgrimage back there with Ike's daughter and we both were appalled to think they had all lived in the tiny little house that was there.

For at least three years, Ike and family lived at Brorein and, because of his personality, he attracted numerous Scouters like me who would spend weekends there, enjoying the lake and the woods and also helping get some of the work done.

During his time there, the camp was known for the signs he made with a router in the shop and placed liberally around the camp. You could not get lost at Camp Brorein.

Ike finally moved to an urban district elsewhere and thus left the camp. It was never quite the same afterwards.

After a move to Texas, Ike retired back home to Colorado. Sadly, he left us at a very young age and is missed by all who knew him.

At any rate, there have been hundreds of these (mostly, if not all) men across the country as long as there have been Scout camps and most of them are fondly remembered by campers, leaders and the members of the profession.

Chapter Ten

Epilogue

It has been more than one hundred years since the BSA was officially chartered and professional Scouters first appeared. Some of these men were great leaders and some were ordinary guys who were called to an unusual profession. A few of them are detailed in these pages.

What will happen to Scouting and professional Scouting in the next hundred years, no one can foretell.

Scouting is changing and has been changing for all of its existence. As this is written, times are hard economically for non-profit organizations and harder in some ways for the BSA because of societal pressure. In spite of many efforts, membership continues to decline, year after year.[143]

The BSA has for some years been assailed by various groups advocating that it should change its interpretation of the Scout Oath and Law to accommodate those of different spiritual beliefs and different interpretations of what constitutes "moral" as set out in the wording of both.

There are valid arguments of fairness and reasonableness, but these codes have been part of Scouting from the beginning. Some members would be offended by changing these interpretations.

Most chartered partner organizations for Scout units are churches and many would object to these changes.[144] On the other hand, some sources of funding have dried up because those sources believe it is wrong not to change.

There has always been an effort to include more members who are not white, middle class boys. The effort has been met with only moderate success. A new effort has begun to include more boys of Hispanic descent, who are under-represented in the BSA. It remains to be seen how this will turn out.

Some calls have been made to include girls in the BSA as is done in the Scouting organizations of some other countries. Girls, of course, are admitted to the Venturing and Learning for Life programs which begin at age 14, but not to the younger boy programs.

The professional Scouter of today is required to deal with these issues and many more in addition to the primary responsibilities they have always had: recruit and train leaders and boys, raise money to operate and give guidance to the volunteer leadership of the movement.

Baden-Powell had in mind a program that would instill certain principles and values in young boys as a foundation for good citizenship so that they would view themselves as valued members of a community and nation. That view has remained constant in a changing world.

Volunteers and parents of Scouts today are asked to contribute money to their local council or to the BSA national organization to supplement the operating budget. Some now question the need for professionals in the numbers they currently exist.

Most are well aware of how much is being spent on executive salaries and benefits and the fact that many volunteers never have any dealings with professionals. An argument can be made for their point of view.

Others are unsatisfied with the direction Scouting is taking at the national level. The members of this profession are well aware of these feelings and sometimes seem oblivious. In any case, the only constant is change and most people don't like change.

There is, too, an element of volunteers around the country who feel that the objective of many professionals today is to create new jobs, bigger councils (many councils around the country are today merging to cover larger geographic regions), and consequently more job stability.

Personally, having been in Boy Scouting since the early 1950s, I question whether it is possible in 21st Century America for a boy to have the same kind of experience in Scouting as I and my friends did then. We can only hope that the Boy Scouts of America will continue to serve the youth of this country as well as it has for the past century.

As this is being written, in 2012, the National Council has announced a new initiative, "Strategic Plan 4-1-1," which is intended to examine and evaluate BSA programs. Having seen many initiatives come and go, experienced Scouters are already wondering what the outcome will be.

There have been a number of these "initiatives" since the beginning: A Ten Year Recruiting Program was instituted in the 1930s under James E. West, which utterly failed to attract more boys. Some wonder whether the men at the top of the Movement have really studied its history and understand what Scouting really stands for. Whether they have or not, translating the principles upon which Scouting was founded into the world of the 21st Century is not an easy task.

In the 1960s a major study showed Scouting was not "in tune with the times" and changes in the program and the uniforms were made. Largely unpopular red berets were official headgear. Advancement requirements were oversimplified and "Skill Awards" were given to Scouts for accomplishing some small part of a rank advancement. The outdoor program was considered unnecessary for "inner city" Scouts, although urban boys had found ways to camp for over half a century.

This initiative coincided with the ultimate boondoggle for Scouting, Boypower '76, seeking to make one American boy in three a Scout, which has been discussed. Ultimately, the major changes of both programs were dropped. Bill Hillcourt, then in retirement, was asked in the 1980s to write a new Boy Scout Handbook which would better reflect the old methods of the program.

In spite of its difficulties, I believe that the Boy Scouts of America is today the only organization that does anything meaningful about teaching really large numbers of boys the values of citizenship, spirituality and personal responsibility. The Mormon Church has used Boy Scouting as its youth program since 1913.

Robert Baden-Powell found a method that attracted boys to his program like flies to honey and it involved camping, hiking, swimming and fun in general.

So far, no one has come up with a better idea. As soon as anyone does, Scouting should immediately adopt it.

For over a hundred years millions of boys have found Scouting to be a meaningful and memorable part of their childhood. Lord Baden-Powell emphasized from the very start that Scouting was a game, played by boys under the guidance of adults. May it always be fun!

In writing this book, I was struck by the number of men in early professional Scouting who lived into really old age. For the most part, these men were active and in good spirits to the very end. I wondered why this was. I can't, of course, give a definitive answer. Maybe some day someone will do a study that will give a better insight.

My thought is that, although the early professionals were mostly hardy, outdoor-loving men, many such men have died younger. They hiked, backpacked, canoed and were generally active in the outdoors. I have come to believe that there is another factor that outweighs a healthy lifestyle: a commitment to service to others. It may sound corny, but the majority of those men who lived and are living into their nineties have a history of dedication to the ideals of Scouting and a desire to see as many youth as possible exposed to those ideals. We know that attitude has a lot to do health, as does a spiritual life. Perhaps it is this dedication to service that causes these men to live so long.

Photo Credits

Page 66

Ernest Thompson Seton, author's collection

Page 67

Daniel Carter Beard, Library of Congress

Page 68

National Executive Board 1915, Library of Congress

Scouts at the Tomb of the Unknown Soldier, Library of Congress

Page 69

G.H. "Obie" Oberteuffer and Mildred, Kenneth Wells. *An Early History of Camp Meriwether*, used by permission

James Austin "Kimo" Wilder, author's collection

Joseph Taylor, Weyrick, David. *To These Things You Must Return*, photographer unknown, believed to be in the public domain

Page 70

Lord Baden-Powell Planting a Tree at Schiff, author's collection

Page 71

Members of the Coordinating Committee, author's collection

1937 Jamboree National Staff, Library of Congress

Page 72

Manor House at Schiff Scout Reservation, author's collection

National Training School Member, author's collection

Lord Rowallan in the Memorial Room at Schiff, author's collection

Page 73

James E. West in the Memorial Room at Schiff, author's collection

Dr. Gunnar Berg and Dr. Arthur Schuck, author's collection

Page 74

William "Green Bar Bill" Hillcourt, 1989, author's collection

Footnotes

1 Men of Schiff, a hymn of the Schiff Scout Reservation, Mendham N.J. Author and origin unknown, although the author was a member of one of the training classes at the National Training School. Sheet music has not been found by the author. Mortimer L. Schiff Scout Reservation, located in central New Jersey, was the principal training site for professional Scouters of the BSA for 50 years. The song became "Friends of Schiff" after the inclusion of women in its training program during the 1970s.

2 MacKinlay Kantor, *For God and My Country*. (The World Publishing Company Cleveland and New York, 1954). Norman Tokar, Director, *Follow Me Boys,* 1966. In the movie, Lem Siddons is a trombone player with a band passing through Hickory, Wisconsin, in the 1930s. During a routine stop, Lem is taken with a young lady he meets briefly and makes a snap decision to remain in Hickory. Later, when no one else will take the job of Scoutmaster for a new troop to be created, Lem steps forward. The decision leads to many years of dedicated service in Scouting and a happy life for Lem.

3 William Hillcourt with Olave, Lady Baden-Powell, *Baden-Powell, Two Lives of a Hero*. (New York, G.P. Putnam's Sons, 1964).

4 For a good summary of this debacle, see Thorson, *History of the Great Southwest Council, 1910-1981.* Referenced are news articles in the following publications:

> *The National Observer*, March 8, 1975
> *U.S. News and World Report*, May 7, 1979
> *The New Republic*, May 19, 1979
> *The Sunday Denver Post*, October 28, 1979

5 E. Elmo St. Lewis in *Official Report of the Second Biennial Conference of Boy Scout Executives,* Boy Scouts of America. 1923. 55

6 McGregor Smith was a business executive in South Florida who was active in Scouting and donated a significant amount of money to the development and promotion of the reservation. He passed away before the first summer camp there opened.

172 Men of Schiff

---

[7] Dave Barry is a Pulitzer Prize winning former humor columnist for the *Miami Herald*, and the author of several humorous books.

[8] United Ways all across the country started cutting funding to the BSA once it was made clear that openly gay leaders and Scouts would not be accepted, a policy that was found to be legal by the U.S. Supreme Court in <u>Boy Scouts of America, et al v. Dale, 530 U.S. 640 (2000)</u>.

[9] Robert Stephenson Smyth Baden-Powell (1877-1941) was, when he died, Robert, Lord Baden-Powell, First Baron of Gilwell, Bt, OM, GCMG, GCVO, KCB. He was a Lieutenant General in the British Army, on the retired list. He held every almost major order and decoration obtainable by a non-royal, from virtually every country around the world. He was also, by acclamation, Chief Scout of the World, a title never held by any other person. He was born, however, into genteel poverty as son of a minister.

[10] Robert S.S. Baden-Powell, *Aids to Scouting*. Originally published by Gale & Polden, Ltd, Aldershot, 1899.

[11] Robert Baden-Powell, *Scouting for Boys*, (The British Scout Association, London, 1908.)

[12] See, e.g., Michael Rosenthal, *The Character Factory, Baden-Powell's Boy Scouts and the Imperatives of Empire*. (New York: Pantheon Books, a division of Random House, Inc.,1984, 1986).

[13] *Scouting for Boys*. Forepiece.

[14] Generally attributed to Baden-Powell.

[15] Rice E. Cochran, *Be Prepared*. (Avon Books, 1952).

[16] Daniel Carter Beard (1850-1941) was an American icon in the early 20th Century. He was an artist, author and the founder of The Sons of Daniel Boone, a pre-Scouting organization for boys. Ernest Thompson Seton (1860-1946) was an author, artist and naturalist. He was the founder of The Birchbark Roll, a pre-Scouting organization for boys.

[17] *Scouting Personnel, A Manual of Human Resources for Local Council Leaders*. (Division of Personnel, Boy Scouts of America, 1937).

[18] *Scouting Personnel*, 1.

[19] Boy Scouts of America, *The Official Handbook for Boys*. (New York, Boy Scouts of America, Doubleday, Page & Co., 1911)

[20] Boy Scouts of America, *Handbook for Scout Masters Boy Scouts of America*, (New York, Boy Scouts of America, 1913).

[21] Although "Scout Executive" has always been the title for the principal executive of a council, and lower ranking staff have held other titles over the years, the term Scout Executive is frequently applied to any professional Scouter.

[22] Ernest Thompson Seton, *Wild Animals I have Known*, (New York, Charles Scribner's Sons, 1912). Some sources say it was originally written and published in 1898, but the author has not been able to verify this.

[23] William D. Murray, *The History of the Boy Scouts of America.* (New York, Boy Scouts of America, 1937). 59-63.

[24] For a good discussion of what happened between Seton and B-P prior to *Scouting for Boys*, see David C. Scott and Brendan Murphy, *The Scouting Party*, (Dallas, TX, Red Honor Press, 2010), especially Chapter Four.

[25] The Silver Buffalo was authorized in 1926 and was designed to emulate the British Silver Wolf Award. It is still the highest award of the BSA. The Silver Antelope Award is given by the National Council, BSA, for service to one of the Regions of the BSA and the Silver Beaver is given by the National Council for service to local councils. All are national awards and are given annually in relatively small numbers. For many years, the awards have been given only to volunteers or to professionals who have been retired or separated for some years and continued to contribute to Scouting after their retirement.

[26] *2d Biennial Conference*, 68.

[27] *2d Biennial Conference*, 216.

[28] Boy Scouts of America, *Scouting Personnel, A Manual of Human Resources for Local Council Leaders.* (Division of Personnel, Boy Scouts of America, 1937).

[29] Murray, 88.

[30] Wilbur F. Creighton, Jr. and Leland R. Johnson, *Boys Will Be Men, Middle Tennessee Scouting Since 1910.* (Nashville, TN, Middle Tennessee Council, BSA, 1983) 37.

[31] Creighton and Johnson, 39-40.

[32] According to the BSA's official spokesman, Greg Shields, in 2007. This represents one professional for every 171 volunteers or one for every 657 youth members. *Deseret News*, Salt Lake City Utah, November 11, 2007.

[33] *Handbook for Scout Masters,* 14.

[34] *Handbook for Scout Masters*, 12.

[35] *Scouting Personnel*, 84 et seq.

[36] *2d Biennial Conference*, 107-118.

[37] See, e.g., http://www.adirondackalmanack.com/2010/05/tracing-scoutings-origins-to-silver-bay-on-lake-george.html. A documentary video is available from various sources.

[38] Robert Peterson in *Scouting Magazine*, October 1998, "The Way It Was, The BSA's forgotten founding father."

39   Janice A. Petterchak, *Lone Scout, W.D. Boyce and American Boy Scouting,* (Janice A. Petterchak, 2003).
40   Paul W. Lewis, *Scouting in Iowa–The Values Endure.* (Mid-Iowa Council, BSA, 1999) 48-50.
41   Edward L. Rowan, M.D., *To Do My Best, James E. West and the History of the Boy Scouts of America,* (Edward Rowan, M.D., 2005).
42   *The Official Handbook for Boys,* 15.
43   Ray R. Matoy, *Thunderbird Tracks, Early History of the Will Rogers Council, BSA,* (Stillwater, OK, Prairie Imprints, undated), 69.
44   Proceedings of the 5th National Training Conference (NTC) 1928, page 246. As cited in Rowan, 83.
45   Rowan, 87-89.
46   Rowan, 93-94.
47   Murray, generally. Rowan, 89, 197, 208.
48   *The New York Times,* July 15, 1957.
49   Boy Scouts of America, *Regional Executives of the BSA, 1920-1968,* (New Brunswick, NJ, 1968).
50   Sources include: Ancestry.com; Order of the Arrow, Boy Scouts of America, *The Silver Arrowhead, Volume 2, Number 2,* Summer, 2009; Elfinwild Church, *The Call,* June, 2010. Http://Elfinwildchurch.org.
51   William Hillcourt, wrote the 1948 edition of *Handbook for Boys,* the Boy Scout handbook, printed in numerous editions by the Boy Scouts of America. Along with James E. West, Hillcourt wrote the 1st Edition of the *Scout Fieldbook,* published by the BSA in 1948. He also wrote all or parts of other editions of these books.
52   Lowell Thomas, *With Lawrence in Arabia,* (London, Hutchinson, 1924). A later edition came out in the 1960s, updated on account of the popularity of the movie about Lawrence, starring Peter O'Toole.
53   Information on Goodman taken in part from: Nelson R. Block, *A Thing of the Spirit: The Life of E. Urner Goodman,* (Irving, TX, Boy Scouts of America 2000).
54   Block, 28-29.
55   The rituals of the Order of the Arrow are "secret" insofar as members don't reveal them to nonmembers within Scouting. Since the members include youth, all such ceremonies are available to leaders, parents and members of the public who need to be aware of what is going on.
56   Mic-O-Say was founded in 1925 at Camp Brinton, near Agency, Indiana, by H. Roe Bartle, Scout Executive of what is

today the Pony Express Council, BSA. Firecrafter is discussed elsewhere. Like OA, both are based on customs and traditions of Native Americans.

57   Venturing is currently the program for youth, male and female, age 14-21.

58   http://www.kosharehistory.org/dancers.html.

59   Bill Hillcourt later received the Distinguished Eagle Award of the BSA and is listed as an Eagle Scout, based on his earning the Danish Knights Scout Award.

60   Boy Scouts of America, *Handbook for Patrol Leaders,* Boy Scouts of America. Originally published in 1929, it was written by Hillcourt until his retirement. The book is still updated and printed by the BSA.

61   Boy Scouts of America, *The Patrol Method, Patrol Helps for the Scoutmaster.* (New York, Boy Scouts of America, 1938).

62   Conversations with the author, ca. 1987-1988.

63   Lady Baden-Powell said at an evening campfire to all listeners at the BSA National Jamboree in Idaho in 1969 that the British Scouts had done some "silly things."

64   Exactly how Roosevelt and Wilder became friends is uncertain, but both moved in the society of New York during the early 20th Century. The friendship is evidenced by both the access Wilder had to Roosevelt when he was Assistant Secretary of the Navy and by letters from Roosevelt to Wilder (with a salutation of "Dear Jimmy,") when he was president.

65   Kinau Wilder, *Wilders of Waikiki,* (Honolulu, Topgallant Publishing Co, 1978).

66   James Austin Wilder, *Jack-Knife Cookery,* (New York, E.P. Dutton & Co., Inc., 1929); The *Pine Tree Patrol,* (New York, Boy Scouts of America, 1930).

67   *2d Biennial Conference,* 129.

68   At the level of a district within a council, the highest award is the District Award of Merit. Councils select a class of recipients each year to receive the Silver Beaver, which is presented by the National Council. Regions can award the Silver Antelope award to volunteers who distinguish themselves. The National Council annually selects a handful of volunteers to receive the Silver Buffalo. Only 20-30 have been presented each year since 1926. A full list can be found at www.scouting.org/About/Factsheets/ Silver_Buffalo.aspx. There was an award, The Silver Fawn, for women only for a short time in the 1960s and 1970s, but women today are elected to receive the same awards as men.

69   Joseph Campbell was a professor at Sarah Lawrence College and the author of numerous books, including *The Hero With a Thousand Faces.* He traveled widely and in later life, made a

number of videos and a series with Bill Moyers called *The Power of Myth*, which are still widely available. He died in 1987.

[70]   William S. Worley, "Bartle, H. Roe," in Lawrence O. Christensen, et al., eds., *Dictionary of Missouri Biography* (Columbia: University of Missouri Press, 1999),

[71]   Alpha Phi Omega is a national, coeducational service fraternity, founded on the cardinal principles of leadership, friendship and service. In its early days, it was solely for college men who had been or were presently in Scouting. The fraternity was founded at Lafayette College by Frank Reed Horton in 1925. http://www.apo.org/.

[72]   Thanks to David L. Eby for his kind permission to use his biographical information on H. Roe Bartle. The full article can be found at: http://usScouts.org/honorsociety/lonebear.asp

[73]   Information on Gunnar Berg from Biographical Sketch of Dr. Gunnar Berg, BSA, New Brunswick, NJ, and a list of excerpts from *The Scout Executive* magazine for professional Scouters, 1927-1962.

[74]   James E. Sundergill, *Carry On! The Life Adventures of Joe Davis, former Director of Camping, Philmont Scout Ranch*, (Cimarron, NM, Philmont Staff Association, 2010).

[75]   Information about Joe Davis taken from his obituary in a Frederick MD newspaper as it appears on the Philmont Staff Association website, and Sundergill's *Carry On!*. See http://www.philstaff.com/ for information about the Philmont Staff Association.

[76]   Robert Baden-Powell, *Scouting for Boys*, (The British Scout Association. Originally published in 1908).

[77]   J. Harold Williams, *Scout Trail 1910-1962*. (Rhode Island Boy Scouts and Narragansett Council, BSA, 1964), 6. Membership in 1962 was 26,631 in 545 units. There are fewer members in the council today.

[78]   Williams, 34-35.

[79]   Williams, 40.

[80]   *Regional Executives of the BSA*. Huffman, *Sam Houston Scouts*, 25.

[81]   Biographic material from various sources including: Minor S. Huffman, *Saga of Potato Canyon, A History of the Conquistador Council, BSA*, (Roswell, NM, Conquistador Council, BSA, 1984), and Lawrence R. Murphy, *Philmont, A History of New Mexico's Cimarron Country*, (Albuquerque, NM, University of New Mexico Press, 1972).

[82]   Huffman, *Potato Canyon*, 1.

[83]   Scout camp names are often concocted from Indian names, names of important individuals or geographic areas. I don't know the origin the this camp name, but the one in Central Florida Council, Camp La-No-Che (or Lanoche), was named for Lake Norris, upon which it is situated and Judge Don Cheney, a council pioneer who was instrumental in obtaining the camp property.

[84]   Huffman, *Potato Canyon*, 45-46.

[85]   Minor S. Huffman, *History of Region Nine, Boy Scouts of America 1920-1967*. (Publication not attributed.)

[86]   Huffman, *Potato Canyon*, 196.

[87]   Most of the information on O.A. Kitterman comes from an unpublished "Life Story" put together while Kit was serving as Regional Executive of Region Eight, updated in 1978 and 1992. Authors were: Wayne Nelson, Elmer Ogren, Earl Behred and W.G. "Bill" Fulton. All were Deputy Regional Executives. Kitterman is also referenced in *A Century of Scouting, 100 Years of Boy Scouts in Boston Minuteman Council, BSA*. Edited by Fred O'Connell. (Boston Minuteman Council, BSA, 2009.)

[88]   *Regional Executives of the BSA.*

[89]   *Regional Executives of the BSA.* Recollections and notes from personal interviews with Dick Newcomb by the author in 2008.

[90]   Now Tuskegee University, Tuskegee, Alabama. The school was founded by Booker T. Washington, among other African-Americans, in 1881, at a time when education of any kind was difficult to obtain for Southern blacks.

[91]   Sources are: The Historical Marker Database, www.hmdb.org/marker.asp?marker=43356, and *Regional Executives of the Boy Scouts of America, 1920-1968*. Boy Scouts of America. New Brunswick, NJ. 1968.

[92]   Information taken from *Regional Executives of the BSA,* Region Six biographies and news articles compiled at the Childers-Mosby family internet site, http://www.childers-mosby.com/childers-mosby. Various dates. Last updated 2005. Some information from personal knowledge of the author.

[93]   Minor S. Huffman, *Sam Houston Scouts, Diamond Jubilee - 1910 - 1985, Seventy Five Years of History in the Sam Houston Area Council, BSA,* (Houston, TX, Sam Houston Area Council, BSA, 1985) 68.

[94]   Rowan, 85.

[95]   The United States Volleyball Association, www.volleyball.org/fisher.html. Block.

[96]   Creighton and Johnson, 41, et seq.

97   David Weyrick, *To These Things You Must Return, A History of the Manatoc Scout Reservation - Part One, Karl Butler and the Original Manatoc, 1882-1926,* (David Weyrick, 2000,2001) 51-52.

98   *2d Biennial Conference,* 474.

99   There are discrepancies among news reports and histories as to the number of people who drowned. It may have been six, seven or eight total.

100   *2d Biennial Conference,* 474.

101   http://www.troop9bsa.org/home/troop-9-history

102   Obituary, *Indianapolis Star or News,* 1947. See: www.firecrafter.org/history/belzer.htm

103   Www.usScouts.org/profbvr/firecrafter/hist1.html

104   What is generally called the Civil War (1860-1865) in the U.S. was not a civil war at all. A civil war is defined as two groups competing to govern the same country. The War Between the States was an attempt for one group of states to separate from the union of the states.

105   William Hairston, *The History of the National Capital Area Council, Boy Scouts of America.* (Washington, National Capital Area Council, BSA, 1998).

106   *Stars and Stripes* is a Department of Defense-authorized daily newspaper distributed overseas for the U.S. military community. Editorially independent of interference from outside its own editorial chain-of-command, it provides commercially available U.S. and world news and objective staff-produced stories relevant to the military community in a balanced, fair, and accurate manner. By keeping its audience informed, Stars and Stripes enhances military readiness and better enables U.S. military personnel and their families stationed overseas to exercise their responsibilities of citizenship. - Revised DoD Directive 5122.11

107   Will Rogers was a humorist and an American legend in the early Twentieth Century. He was an authentic cowboy, a vaudevillian and political commentator. His name was a household word in the 1920s and 1930s. Rogers was killed in an airplane crash off Alaska in 1935.

108   *Pawhuska Daily Journal-Capital,* February 8, 1970. The Chronicles of Oklahoma. Fall, 2005. Pawhuska, Oklahoma: Home to America's First Boy Scout Troop. Written by Joe D. Haines, Jr. Information about Transatlantic Council, BSA, and life as an American military dependant in Germany during the late 1950s is from the author's personal knowledge. There is an internet site for the council: www.tac-bsa.org/

109   Lagrange News, Lagrange, Georgia, January 13, 2012. Andrea Lovejoy, Contributing Editor. As found on: www.lagrangenews.com/view/full_story/17124206/article-Willie-

Fuller--LaGrange%E2%80%99s-Tuskegee-
Airman?instance=secondary_news_left_column
[110]   Warren R. Hauff, *Fun and Service, A History of the Boy Scouts of America in the Miami Valley Council.* (Dayton, Ohio. Miami Valley Council, BSA, 1970). Illustrated by Eagle Scout Milt Caniff) 18.
[111]   Hauff, 23-24.
[112]   In the days when railroads were the main means of long-distance travel, there were special cars that offered sleeping accommodations for overnight travel, at a higher cost. They were like dormitories, with curtains for the bunks, and were called Pullman cars, after the original designer, George Pullman. If you couldn't afford a Pullman for a long trip, you just slept in your seat.
[113]   Hauff, 63-64.
[114]   Hauff, 83-84.
[115]   Cub Scouting today accepts boys aged six to 11½. Of the approximately 2.7 million youth members of Scouting, Cubs represent a little over half. Since the Webelos program of Cub Scouting takes older boys into much of what Boy Scouts do, like camping, and can retain them until they are almost twelve, many boys simply "burn out" on Scouting without ever trying the Boy Scout program. Additionally, the sheer numbers of boys in that program place a huge burden on local council facilities like Scout camps.
[116]   Information about Camp Manotoc and Karl Butler taken from Weyrick, *To These Things You Must Return,* cited above.
[117]   Information about Dwight Ramsey taken from Weyrick and *Regional Scout Executives of the Boy Scouts of America,* cited above.
[118]   P.V. Thorson, *History of the Great Southwest Council, BSA, or Scouting Marches on to the Better Life!* (Self published, 1982).
[119]   Thorson, 4-5.
[120]   Thorson, 112.
[121]   Huffman, *Potato Canyon,* 87.
[122]   Robert L. Ripley was a newspaper cartoonist. In the 1920s he began to specialize in publishing odd and unusual happenings. See http://www.ripley .com for information.
[123]   http://familytreemaker.genealogy.com/users/h/o/d/Walter-G-Hodge/GENE2-0004.html
[124]   W. Joseph Wyatt, *Buckskin Boys, A History of the Buckskin Council, 1919-2004,* (Charleston, WVA, Pictorial Histories Publishing Company, 2004).
[125]   Wyatt, 11-13.

[126]   Wyatt, 44-46.

[127]   Wyatt, 49.

[128]   Kenneth Wells, *An Early History of Camp Meriwether*, (Portland, OR, Columbia Pacific Council, BSA, 1984).

[129]   Boy Scout ranks, then and now are: Tenderfoot, Second Class, First Class, Star, Life and Eagle. In the 1970s, the rank of Scout was added for new members and ranked below Tenderfoot.

[130]   Wells, 34. Portland Sea Scouts have continued to excel through the decades into the 21st Century.

[131]   Wells, 45-47. Harry Truman, no relation to the U.S. president of the same name, became quite well known around the country during the build-up to the eruption of the volcano. He refused to move out of his lodge on Spirit Lake and was still there on the morning of the eruption. His body was never found.

[132]   Willard Adams, *My Thirty Years of Scouting*. Privately printed and undated.

[133]   Huffman, *Sam Houston Scouts*, 23-24.

[134]   Information from Frank Ballingers website at http://www.texashideout.tripod.com. Created and maintained by Frank R. Ballinger.

[135]   *1926 Annual, Boy Scouts of Delaware & Montgomery Counties*, Editors Edgar S. Nash and Frank M. Hardy, (Delaware and Montgomery Counties Council, 1927).

[136]   Hillcourt, 376-377.

[137]   The best information found about the exposition itself appears in a well-documented page of Wikipedia.com. Sesquicentennial information is also found on phillyhistory.com.

[138]   Huffman, *History of Region Nine*, 14.

[139]   Huffman, 43.

[140]   Huffman, 183.

[141]   Huffman, 182.

[142]   John J. Foster, *On My Honor, The History of the Lebanon County Council, Boy Scouts of America*. (Lebanon, PA, Lebanon County Historical Society, 1993) 124-125.

[143]   For a balanced discussion of the issues facing the BSA in the early 21st Century, including membership decline, as well as actual numbers and percentage of change, see wikipedia.org/wiki/Boy_Scouts_of_America_membership_controversies. It should be noted that the author does not share the view that decrease in numbers is due primarily to the controversies. There are many demographic and cultural reasons for the decline. It can also be noted that, at the time of this writing, the BSA is considering a policy of allowing chartered partner organizations to set standards, including those of sexual orientation, for the leadership of units they sponsor.

[144] A chartered partner organization in the BSA is a church, club or group of citizens who actually "own" the Scout unit. The partner organization is responsible, most importantly, for the selection and supervision of the leadership of the unit. It also has responsibility for finding a unit meeting place. Each partner organization has a representative who votes on local council matters as a member of its executive board.

Bibliography

Adams, Willard. *My Thirty Years of Scouting*. CA: Privately published. 1955.

Baden-Powell, Robert. *Scouting for Boys*. The Scout Association, London. 1991. (Reprint of original version.)

Block, Nelson R. *A Thing of the Spirit: The Life of E. Urner Goodman*. Irving TX: Boy Scouts of America. 2000.

Boy Scouts of America. *Handbook for Patrol Leaders*. New Brunswick, New Jersey: Boy Scouts of America.

_____. *Handbook for Scout Masters, Boy Scouts of America*. 1913, 1914. Boy Scouts of America.

_____. *The National and World Jamboree in Pictures: The First National Jamboree of the Boy Scouts of America and the Fifth World Jamboree of Scouting*. Boy Scouts of America. 1937.

_____. *Regional Executives of the Boy Scouts of America, 1920-1968*. New Brunswick, NJ: Boy Scouts of America. 1968.

_____. *Scout Field Book*. Boy Scouts of America, New Brunswick, New Jersey.

_____. *Scouting Personnel.* New York: Boy Scouts of America. 1937.

Boy Scouts of America, Delaware and Montgomery Counties. *1926 Annual, Boy Scouts of America, Delaware and Montgomery Counties, 1927.*

Brittain, William J. *The Spirit of Scouting '76*, St. Louis: The St. Lewis Area Council, BSA. 1976.

Clemens, Cyril. *Uncle Dan: The Life Story of Dan Beard*, New York: Thomas Y. Crowell Co. 1942.

Creighton, Wilbur F., Jr. & Leland R. Johnson. *Boys Will Be Men.* Nashville: Middle Tennessee Council, BSA. 1983.

Daniel Boone Council, BSA. *History of the Daniel Boone Council, BSA, 1911-1968.* Reading, PA: Daniel Boone Council. 1968.

Foster, John J. *On My Honor.* Lebanon, PA: Lebanon County Historical Society. 1993.

Four Lakes Council, BSA. *The First Ninety Years, 1912-2002, Four Lakes Council, BSA* 2002. Four Lakes Council, BSA, Madison, WI. 2003.

Hairston, William. *The History of the National Capital Area Council, BSA.* The National Capital Area Council, BSA. 1998.

Hauff, Warren R. *Fun and Service: A History of the Boy Scouts of America in the Miami Valley Council.* Dayton, OH: Miami Valley Council, BSA. 1970.

Hillcourt, William and Olave, Lady Baden-Powell. *Baden-Powell: The Two Lives of a Hero.* New York, N.Y: G.P. Putnam's Sons. 1964

Holland,J. Baron, Editor. *Sixty-two Years of Scouting With Troop 203.* Richard H. Barnes and J. Bartram Holland. 1982.

Huffmann, Minor S. *History of Region Nine, BSA, 1920-1967.* No publication information.

_____. *Saga of Potato Canyon: A History of the Conquistador Council, BSA.* Roswell, NM: Conquistador Council, BSA. 1984.

_____. *Sam Houston Scouts.* Houston: Sam Houston Area Council, BSA, 1985.

Kameroski, Thomas A. *A History of Goose Pond Scout Reservation.* Montdale, PA: T.A. Kameroski. 2007.

Lewis, Paul W. *Scouting in Iowa–The Values Endure.* Mid Iowa Council, BSA. 1999.

Matoy, Ray. *Thunderbird Tracks: Early History of the Will Rogers Council. BSA,* Stillwater, OK: Prairie Imprints. 1987.

Murphy, Lawrence R. *Philmont, A History of New Mexico's Cimarron Country.* Lawrence R. Murphy. 1972.

Murray, William D. *A History of the Boy Scouts of America.* New York, N.Y.: Boy Scouts of America. 1937.

O'Connell, Fred, Editor. *A Century of Scouting.* Boston: Boston Minuteman Council. 2009.

Oursler, Fulton. *The Boy Scout Story.* Garden City, N.Y.: Doubleday and Co, Inc. 1955.

Petterchak, Janice A. *Lone Scout: W.D. Boyce and American Boy Scouting.* Janice A. Petterchak. 2003

Roosevelt Council, BSA. *Outdoor Activities: Roosevelt Council, BSA.* Roosevelt Council, BSA. 1933.

Rosenthal, Michael. *The Character Factory: Baden-Powell's Boy Scouts and the Imperatives of Empire.* New York: Pantheon Books. 1984.

Rowan,Edward L., M.D. *To Do My Best: James E. West and the History of the Boy Scouts of America.* Edward Rowan, M.D. 2005.

Russell Sage Foundation. *Building a Popular Movement.* Russell Sage Foundation, New York. 1944.

Sundergill, James E. *Carry On! The Life Adventures of Joe Davis, Former Director of Camping, Philmont Scout Ranch.* Cimarron, NM: Philmont Staff Association. 2010

Thorson, P.V. *History of the Great Southwest Council 1910-1981.* P.V. Thorson. 1981.

Wells, Kenneth. *An Early History of Camp Meriwether.* Portland, OR: The Columbia Pacific Council, BSA. 1984, 1986

Wilder, Kinau. *Wilders of Waikiki..* Honolulu: Topgallant Publishing,. 1978.

Williams, J. Harold. *Scout Trail: The Story of Scouting in Rhode Island.* Providence, R.I.: Rhode Island Boy Scouts and Narragansett Council, BSA. 1964.

Wills, Chuck. *Boy Scouts of America: A Centennial History.* London, New York, Melbourne, Munich and Delhi: DK Publishing.

Weyrick, David. *To These Things You Must Return: A History of the Manatoc Scout Reservation - Part One: Karl Butler and the Original Manatoc.* 2000, 2001.

Wolverton, David Alan. *Images of America, Monmouth Council Boy Scouts,* Charleston, SC: Arcadia Publishing. 2003.

Wyatt, W. Joseph. *Buckskin Boys: A History of the Buckskin Council, 1919-2004.* Charleston, WV: Pictorial Histories Publishing Co., Inc. 2004.

Index

Made in the USA
Monee, IL
23 December 2023

50439188R00125